James

Happy Birthday

L

D0708021

ed

7/4/93.

MY LORD'S

MY LORD'S

*A Celebration of the
World's Greatest Cricket Ground*

EDITED BY TIM HEALD

Willow Books
Harper Collins

Willow Books
William Collins Sons & Co., Ltd
London · Glasgow · Sydney · Auckland · Toronto · Johannesburg

First published in 1990
© MCC and Tim Heald 1990

Illustrations by Colin Wheeler

A CIP CATALOGUE RECORD FOR THIS BOOK IS AVAILABLE FROM THE BRITISH LIBRARY

ISBN 0 00 218363 3

Designed by Judith Gordon
Set in Linotron Sabon by Phoenix Photosetting, Chatham, Kent
Printed and bound in Great Britain by
Mackays of Chatham PLC, Chatham, Kent

Contents

CONTENTS

Editor's
Introduction

TIM HEALD

For any properly brought up Englishman of a certain age the voice of E. W. Swanton carries an almost magical authority. For one like me, whose earliest first-class cricket was experienced vicariously as my friends and I huddled round the enormous crackling wireless in the library at Connaught House School just outside Bishop's Lydeard near Taunton, that voice still has the power to take one back to childhood. Those mellifluous bluff phrases describing the doings of Hutton and Compton, Miller and Lindwall were as much a part of my education as *Kennedy's Latin Primer* or *The Book of Common Prayer*. Indeed, blasphemous though it may seem to those not similarly educated, you could say there are men alive in England for whom the voice of Swanton is, as near as dammit, the voice of God.

It was therefore disconcerting to hear it coming down the telephone from Sandwich in Kent where he lives, mainly, I believe, because it is so convenient for Royal St George's Golf Club and not too far from various places where Kent play cricket. The voice was well over eighty now but it was unmistakeable. The line from Kent was just as crackly as the old school wireless so the sensation of being transported back to the 1950s was all but complete, except for the fact that the voice was not addressing the nation but me alone.

He was asking me to edit a book about Lord's for the Marylebone Cricket Club. It would be an anthology. The running title would be *My Lord's*. It was simply a question of commissioning a whole lot of chaps – and conceivably a chappess or two – to write something original about their love affair with the ground. He mentioned some financial figures, rather low financial figures, but by now I was scarcely listening. This was not an offer, it seemed to me, that one could possibly refuse. My cricketing career had never progressed beyond that far-off day when I opened for my college social team at Great Tew and was bowled for nought. But oh, to have captained MCC at Lord's and now, at last, albeit only in a literary sense, the summons had come. And from Swanton himself.

9

Some places are more than just places and one of these is Lord's. A cricket ground for a true cricket-lover is never just a cricket ground, but some are more prosaic than others and there are some which do not lift the soul. It would be a curmudgeonly cricketing person, however, who did not feel some *frisson* of excitement at the idea of the Mecca of cricket, that still spacious oasis of green and wrought iron, linseed oil and blanco, which lounges in glorious anachronism among the high-rise flats, the private hospitals and the tourist hotels of London's St John's Wood. Even someone alien to cricket would surely sense that Lord's is special.

Cricket is the most literary of sports and Lord's the most literary of its palaces. Ever since it stopped being a vegetable garden and turned to cricket in 1887 it has been lauded in prose and verse. Many of these celebrations are rather awful, but some are classics of their kind. Whole books have been devoted to the place and Benny Green has produced an anthology of Lord's writing which runs to over 450 densely packed pages.

I toyed at first with the idea of including some of the classics: the great Francis Thompson poem ('O My Hornby and My Barlow Long Ago, Long Ago'); Sir Spencer Ponsonby-Fane's 1914 introduction to Ashley-Cooper's book, in which he remembered a one-roomed Pavilion surrounded by laurels and 'Mr Benjamin Aislabie, the Secretary of the Club, a big fat man over 20 stone in weight, fussing about with a red book in which he was entering subscriptions for some desired match, of which the funds of the Club could not afford the expense'; V. S. Naipaul's account of the 1963 West Indies' Test; Robertson-Glasgow's return to a Lord's where he saw 'the same spectator whom I always see on my first day at Lord's. He was waiting for his brother, who is always late.'

Of course any definitive Lord's book must contain these and other gems, but they have all been anthologized time and again already and I decided, perhaps recklessly, that I would concentrate on new stuff. I say 'concentrate' because it isn't as simple as it sounds. What do you do, for instance, when you approach Harold Pinter and he offers you an article published some years ago but now almost forgotten? After some thought I decided to use it. Or when William Douglas-Home produces a poem he first wrote more than sixty years ago after watching an Eton and Harrow match as a schoolboy? I've used that, too. There are a very few other pieces which I know are not brand new, but in the main I think they are, even though a few contributors may have pulled something from their bottom drawer without my realizing it. I'm fairly sure I recognize one or two of the jokes in some articles, but on the whole a good joke bears repeating.

Team selection is always controversial and I am well aware that this will strike many of you as a pretty rum lot. Good. I would hate to be predictable, but at the risk of sounding defensive I would like to pre-empt one or two criticisms. Not everyone shares my attitude to Swanton, Lord's and the MCC (I know putting 'the' in front of MCC is often supposed to be a solecism but I prefer this usage). Whereas I regarded Swanton's request as a command to which the answer 'no' was not just not expected but actually impossible, others seemed to think that it was a take it or leave it situation. One or two even considered the money (not great, I agree) was insulting. A sign of the times, I'm afraid. There is obviously a literary Gattingism abroad.

One or two candidates ruled themselves out on more acceptable grounds. Melvyn Bragg, for instance, would have taken part if asked to write about Headingley. And I specially liked John Major's two letters. Despite having just been invited by Mrs Thatcher to become her Foreign Secretary he said that mine was 'the nicest invitation I have received for some time'. He added, however, that 'the overwhelming majority of my cricketing memories are of The Oval since I lived next door to it during the 1950s, when Surrey won seven successive Championships with what was probably the greatest county team ever (well, in my view anyway)'.

Once or twice my information was awry. I was told as an absolute article of faith that the actor and writer Anthony Sher was an avid cricket fan and constantly to be found on top of the Warner Stand or in the Tavern. When his postcard came, however, it said, 'I am unable to contribute to your book since I have never watched a game of cricket in my life.'

I have tended to select writers with a passion for cricket rather than cricketers with a passion for writing because I wanted something which held up as a piece of literature, however ephemeral. For the same reason I'm afraid I have resisted various attempts to include men whose knowledge of the game, usually some aspect of administration, might be encyclopedic but whose prose I felt would be less than deathless.

I asked for each piece to be between a thousand and two thousand words, crisp and to the point, elegant without being too elegiac, and firmly rooted in first-hand personal experience. I was petrified of essays on the soaring feeling one experiences when passing through the Grace Gates or euphoric pieces about the halcyon days of 1947 ('O My Edrich and My Compton Long Ago, Long Ago'). I longed for truly original pieces of writing about the greatest of all cricket grounds.

Whether I have succeeded is for the reader to decide. I have been deliberately not definitive; sometimes wilfully whimsical, occasionally subversive. This is a book of serendipity, a bedside companion of disparate thoughts and opinions, anecdotes and musings by a group of writers who have only one thing in common. They all, in their very different ways, 'have a thing about Lord's'. Like any anthology it has some of the characteristics of the curate's egg. At least, most readers will think it has. But I have gone on long enough. It is time for play to begin and for you to see for yourself.

William Douglas-Home and J. L. Carr are my idea of a perfect opening pair – an elegant amateur and a gritty northern professional, though like all such analogies this one is shot through with fallacies. Douglas-Home, as his prodigious output of theatrical comedies so amply demonstrates, is a thoroughgoing professional, while Carr can be as elegant in his style as any Gower or Woolley. Douglas-Home's famous plays such as The Reluctant Debutante *and* The Chiltern Hundreds *are stuffed with obvious cricketers. His elder brother, Lord Home, was Prime Minister but also, more significantly, President of MCC. The following poem is a childhood relic of more than half a century ago.*

'A Glorious Game, Say We'

WILLIAM DOUGLAS-HOME

These lines were composed at Eton College after going to the match against Harrow at Lord's in the 1920s.

Though we sit tired out by the hours of play
When the shadows of evening fall
We have watched through the dancing heat of the day
The struggle 'twixt bat and ball
For we love the changes and chances of cricket
Though the bat succeeds or fails
Though the ball is striking the fatal wicket
Or the white pavilion rails
For cricket's a glorious game, say we
And cricket will never cease to be

Yes, cricket will live till the trumpet trumps
From the wide pavilioned sky
And time, the umpire, lays low the stumps

As his scythe goes sweeping by
Till the mighty seed of humanity fails
At the light of another birth
And God stoops down to remove the bails
From the dark deserted earth
Yes, cricket's a glorious game, say we
And cricket will live in eternity

J. L. Carr's novels include two that made the Booker Prize short list and A Season in Sinji, *which Matthew Engel has described as 'the best cricket-based novel I have read'.*

Looking for Lord

J. L. CARR

Although we keep quiet about it, even before 1974's outrageous cessions to Durham, Lincolnshire and, unforgivably, Lancashire, Yorkshire was a loose confederation of counties. There was Holderness, Allertonshire, Craven, Howdenshire, Hallam, Richmondshire and Buckrose. It was from the coal, steel and wool towns of Hallamshire and Craven (the now lost West Riding) that major cricketers – Tunnicliffe, Emmott, Hirst, Rhodes, Sutcliffe and Verity – were recruited.

The East and North Ridings were never fertile breeding grounds. Their natives are milder folk, less aggressive, less inclined to speak their minds disconcertingly. Their twang is not so flat, their wit more tongue-in-cheek. They are Yorkshire all right, but don't everlastingly tell you so. By and large, from Holderness to Richmondshire is farming country, moors, small villages, large mansions and market towns like the one with a chill east wind of a name – Thirsk.

Thirsk lies in the Vale of Mowbray. Its railway station on the old LNER main line is at the back end of the racecourse and a good half mile from the Monday Marketplace, a big cobbled square. Off it and up Kirkgate, Thomas Lord was born on 23 November 1755 (the same day that John Wesley visited the town).

In those days No. 23, a single-storeyed thatched cottage, seems to have been joined internally to both its neighbours. In fact, it is highly likely that the Lord family had to make do with no more than a couple of rooms. It was all a far cry from the Long Room at Lord's.

Nowadays the house has another floor and its roof is pantiled.

MCC's tablet above the front door gives Thomas's basic history – the years of his birth and death, and a terse account of the several flittings of his eponymous London memorial.

But the general run of folk don't make as much fuss of the town's best-known son as one might suppose they should. A Mr Sykes growled that he was 'nobbut a market gardener good at growing grass' and, even less kindly, went on to describe him as 'nowt but a jumped-up property developer, the sort who, these days, would be fettling up golf courses up and down the M4 for these here Japs'. So, really, it is not surprising that The Birthplace has to treble-up with the town's museum and an English Heritage-funded tourist office. And, when I asked if a Thomas Lord Heritage Trail was planned, I was told that his only trail unforgivably led Down South. Not even his desertion at the tender age of ten earned him remission from this heavy sentence. So the Lord Trail begins and ends on his front doorstep. ('But we are thinking about a James Herriot Trail . . . he lives just up the road. *He's* stayed put.')

Charitably, a local-history hand-out rallies to his cause. This says, 'People suppose that the famous cricket field gets its name from some aristocratic connection. Not so. It is Lord's with an apostrophe, indicating the possessive case. Our Lord was not a lord: he was a farm servant's son.'

We now must fall back upon Oral Recollection. (This refuge for cornered local historians is always charmingly enchanted ground.) Here we discover that 'his father was not a *proper Yorkshireman*. In fact [in lower tones], he even may have been a Scotsman who lost all but life, limb and honour in the Jacobite Cause and fled for shelter to an enclave of Roman Catholics who worshipped in the chapel at South Kilvington Hall. Squire Bell set him to work on his market garden behind the Three Tuns and, to cut down cash payments, knocked the rent of No. 23 off his wages.' And another oral recollector revealed that the Lords were Chartists. But, as this would have meant the family were anticipating this radical outcry by a hundred years, he may have meant 'Papists'.

So, in Thirsk, Thomas Lord remains a shadowy, a marginal figure. Now, in passing, there is a moral here. For those of us who feel that posterity may wish to know more about us, it plainly is not enough just to leave behind a cricket ground, even one so grand as Lord's. We must see to it that written records of the sort likely to do us credit are left and lodged in a safe place. In fact, the sensible thing would be to have them carved in hard-wearing stone and fixed firmly into a stout wall unlikely ever to be threatened by planning permission. MCC's tablet at No. 23 is a step in the right direction, but it is too little, too late.

Yet Thirsk is not alone in its neglect: *The Dictionary of National Biography* has forgotten him, too. A *Henry* Lord may be found there. He was no more than a £60-a-year East India Company curate whose sermons were so unsustaining that the directors irritably voted him £20 'to buy more books'. There is a *Percy* Lord, who fell at the Defeat of Purwan and whose father was chaplain to an Institution for Decayed Irish Gentlewomen. And there is another Thomas Lord (*c.* 1796), who did little to earn his place except to be 'last heard of near The Obelisk'. Fourth and finally – *John Keast* Lord. He first appears as a castaway, then (dressed in the costume of a Minnesota trapper) as a popular lecturer, and terminally he disappears, 'led astray by his convivial tastes. It is said that he was the son of Edward Lord.' '*It is said that he was the son of* . . .' – this always is an interesting speculation.

Earlier, I mentioned a visit paid to Thirsk by John Wesley on the day of Thomas Lord's birth, but I also should have revealed that, as the evangelist rode under the Hambleton Hills and whilst in the neighbourhood of Sutton-under-Whitestone Cliff, there was a violent earth tremor and several large boulders rattled down the hillside across his path. He rode on to the town. But his *Journal* does not record any preaching there. All he says is, 'The place is full of cock-fighters and curious swearers.' So why did he come? On that particular day? Surely this should be looked into by Thirsk's local historians. Their search might well begin back in 1736 and along Georgia's Susquehanna River. . . .

(But history is full of these mysteries. For instance, no one ever has satisfactorily explained to me why Mrs Emma Locksley, landlady of the new Lord's Tavern, came to blow up the house, her sister-in-law and herself. We were not following on after the Australians that day.)

Yet my impression was that, all in all, Thirsk is quietly proud of Thomas Lord but uneasy that it is able to tell pilgrims so little about his ten-year stay. They have learnt from TV politicians, however, and no longer blush to answer not the question they have been asked but the one they would like to have been asked. So I was told about George Freeman, a Thirsk auctioneer who, between 1867 and 1871, often in company with Tom Emmott, on seven occasions for the county bowled unchanged through an innings. I was told that he had been taught his peculiar delivery by Canon Owen of Boroughbridge. (And this must have been a very peculiar delivery indeed. Not only was it fast but it shot across the pitch and, 'even after striking the stumps, still spun violently'.)

And then, what about George Macaulay, whose mother kept the Fleece Hotel? Surely I had heard of George? *He played at Lord's.* Did I not recall the 1926 Headingley Test when A. W. Carr won the toss and put the Australians in to make 494? George's 76 during the follow-on saved the game (but not Carr's captaincy). And this is not Oral Recollection. This is confirmed by *Wisden.* Nevertheless, George Macaulay's memorial is neither that desperate innings nor his 1773 wickets (for 17 runs apiece). His garland is forever green because of that sardonic answer given to Edgar Oldroyd's enquiry as to how he was liking a long spell against a stiff wind. 'It's like bowling up t'bloody cellar steps,' he said.

'And let's not forget Louis Rider,' I was urged, and now I listened with great attention indeed, for Lou was the son of Lot Rider, landlord of my childhood home. When I was a small boy I would look across the meadow to watch a lonely figure slinging rearing deliveries at a hanging straw sack. Not enough sympathy is given by writers to that vast host who *almost* won a place in county sides, who were weighed in the balance and found wanting. Louis was such a one. His sad little record tells all: 4 wickets for 151 and one innings of 1 run.

I, too, left Thirsk when I was ten and, in the 1930s, was living close to West Meon in Hampshire, unknowingly near to the last home of my fellow townsman. It is a village by a trout stream and in a pass of the downs. In those days the pub was the New Inn. And all I remember was a damp little church on a winter afternoon. But, when I returned fifty years later, West Meon had moved further than Thirsk along the Thomas Lord Heritage Trail. The New Inn has become the Thomas Lord Hotel and its landlord displays seventy-three county and club ties, sets of cricketing cigarette cards, and a framed letter from Sir Jack Hobbs.

But the North Riding town yet can trump that Hampshire ace. Thirsk has a poem and, as everyone with his heart in the right place knows, even more than cricket, verse is England's true glory. This splendid salute was written by Ronald Scriven, the poet once employed by *The Yorkshire Post*, and here it is:

> On Thirsk Cricket Field the sward
> Was, I'm positive, adored
> By its son, one Thomas Lord
> Born in Kirkgate once on a day.
> Later on, he made his way
> To London and became renowned
> For sacrosanct Lord's Cricket Ground.

To follow Douglas-Home and Carr in I have decided to pack Swanton, Arlott, Johnston and Woodcock in together. The sight of these four coming in to write should strike the fear of God into any imaginable opposition, for they are the great veterans of contemporary cricket commentating. E. W. Swanton, familiarly known as 'Jim', played cricket for Middlesex and MCC, has twice taken his own team to the West Indies, and has been president of Kent. He covered twenty Test tours for The Daily Telegraph *and was a BBC cricket commentator from 1934 to 1975.*

Sixty Years On

E. W. SWANTON

MCC and Lord's have meant much to many, but comparatively few have had the good fortune to enjoy so close an association for so long. Having played my candidate qualifying matches, I was elected in 1936: but my regular attendance as a cricket writer began just over sixty years ago. I even have a clear recollection of seeing the Middlesex–Surrey match of 1921 which ended in Middlesex retaining the Championship they had won in Plum Warner's last match the previous year.

Newcomers to Lord's are usually taken by a certain atmosphere experienced, perhaps, from the time of their entry via the Grace Gates, dignified yet not grandiose, like the inscription on the central column. The Committee had difficulty in deciding between several suggestions, in English, Latin and even Greek – which, if adopted, might have caused the Old Man to pluck at his celestial beard a bit. In the end Stanley Jackson came up with all that needed to be said: 'To William Gilbert Grace, the great cricketer.'

There was and still is much about Lord's that is understated. The flowerbeds which first greet the visitor beneath 'Q', henceforth to be known, properly enough, as the Allen Stand, suggest one is not entering a functional arena, as does the memorial garden to the great Lord Harris behind the south end of the Pavilion, which when I first knew it was a lawn tennis court. North of the Pavilion lies a post-war improvement very much in character, the quiet Coronation Garden, much favoured for picnics on big match days.

The Pavilion itself, which dominates the architecture of the ground and, pray God, always will, speaks of Victorian certitude, a focus of imperial cricket when it was built (in 7 months!) in 1889–90 and today a symbol of the permanence of MCC and cricket in a changing world. It is massive, yes, but with good lines and proportions, scarcely overbearing. He must be a Philistine who feels no emotion on first entering the Long Room. When I became responsible, comparatively recently, for its treasures of pictures and cricketana, as chairman of the Arts and Library Sub-committee, I felt no less a thrill than when I first knew the room so many years before.

Likewise, what cricketer passing through on to the field for the first time cannot be at least dimly conscious that he is treading where great men from W.G. onwards have trod before him? Certainly not I as in June 1935 I went out to bat against Indian Gymkhana (at number five following Denis Compton, 10, and Bill Edrich, 60. Against the formidable Amar Singh I made a sketchy 7!).

The Grandstand has always been a less than satisfactory building since for its size it contains the minimum number of seats. Yet it is at least comely and its surmounting weather vane showing Old Father Time with his scythe putting on the bails (a present from the architect, Sir Herbert Baker) has become a worldwide talisman denoting Lord's and the game. I reported my first and, for me, finest Test in 1930 in a temporary press box annexe at ground level beneath the Grandstand.

The look of the rest of the ground has altered greatly since I first knew it, but the architects concerned – of the Tavern complex and the new Mound Stand – have steered clear of any stadium effect. The Mound, with those graceful pinnacles, has earned the approval of the Prince of Wales no less. So much for the ground itself.

As to the people, the indelible impression which I retain is of the courtesy and charm shown to me by older men. For me they expressed all that is meant by the fellowship of cricket, a philosophy which is still to be found in these more urgent, pressured days – notably among schoolmasters and professional coaches, and, not least, among the present Secretariat and staff at Lord's.

My first remembrance concerns not the Pavilion but the press box – the friendships one found there and withal the decorum. The senior residents were mostly not members of MCC, but none were more deeply rooted in the game's traditions than the partners in the Cricket Reporting Agency, who became successive Editors of *Wisden*: Charles Stewart Caine, who fathered me in early days in the Press Club; Sydney Southerton (son of James, who played in the first of all Tests, at Melbourne in 1876–7); and Hubert Preston. I never met a more delightful man than old Stewart Caine. Sydney, a popular fellow whom Percy Chapman made an honorary member of his 1928–9 team in Australia, died at The Oval as he sat down following an after-dinner speech but not before he had contributed to *Wisden* a masterly appraisal and judicial condemnation of the 'Bodyline' tour. He was succeeded by Preston (father of a later Editor, Norman), who wielded an expanding black ear-trumpet – 'Don't shout, boy, I'm not deaf.' He was, very.

Some cricket correspondents were, of course, MCC members, and they were often kind enough to introduce me into the Pavilion. One was Colonel Philip Trevor, CBE, whose name plus honour spread nicely under the headline across the *Daily Telegraph* column. He, too, had a graver affliction in his job, being in old age extremely short-sighted. I could help him in this on cricket grounds, as his daughter also did with me in rugger press boxes. Philip had managed the second MCC tour to Australia, that of 1907–8, the first of Jack Hobbs's five visits. He was caustic when necessary but liked to find a kind word for everyone, down to, 'Good, too, was so-and-so,' without specifying further.

The *Morning Post* correspondent – doubling, believe it or not, in several years during those more relaxed, less critical days as Chairman of the Test Selectors – was P. F. Warner, who in 1937 became Sir Pelham. When he signed me into the Pavilion he showed his red membership pass to the door-keeper, saying to me, 'I've never gone through these doors without showing it.' It was a little lesson in good manners that I've practised at Lord's and all over the world ever since.

The press box then was above the professionals' changing-rooms at the north end of the Pavilion. It so happened I was the last man to work there on the last evening of the season of 1957, before its conversion during the winter into the Secretarial Offices, and I thought of these early heroes of mine – and of Cardus and Robertson-Glasgow and Howard Marshall and others – as I bade it farewell.

This brings me to the MCC staff. They all breathed the spirit of the place, a seemingly happy band, unified by affection for Ronny Aird, the Assistant Secretary. There were Dick and Joe Gaby, sons of old Dick who served MCC in numerous capacities – taking charge of the members' horses and carriages, for instance – from boyhood in 1875 until his retirement sixty-three years later. 'Young Dick' was on the staff for forty-four years, finishing as ground superintendent, while Joe was in charge of the Pavilion. A thoroughly unique century!

The caterer was George Portman, who not only supplied lunches (members 2s. 6d., guests 3s. 6d.) and dinners to order but also ran the bakery under the Mound Stand and the Lord's cake shop giving on to St John's Wood Road. George was a high-class chef – I can still taste his fresh-baked bath buns, the recipe for which is doubtless lost along with that for Hatfield, the perfect Pimm-like drink, reddish in colour, the ingredients for which were so secret that they were lost beyond recovery during the war.

Portman served a mere forty-eight years at Lord's, a trifle compared with the sixty-five of his fellow Cockney, Jimmy Cannon, the head clerk, a ruddy-cheeked little man with an invariable flower in his buttonhole, who had the facility, after weighing up the weather and all relevant factors, to predict with uncanny accuracy the size of the crowd – much to the advantage of his friend the caterer.

I must not forget Mrs Barrow, who reigned – and that is the word – over the Pavilion Long Bar, a lady of awesome dignity who with a toque on her head would have looked the spitting image of Queen Mary. In a rare relaxed moment she was reported as remarking: 'Say what you like about the Middlesex members, they're a bit more generous than the MCC ones.' The reference was thought to be to the occasional offer of a glass of port, enjoyed discreetly out of sight. Anxious enquiries after the war disclosed that at one time she was the only resident of her bombed street in Peckham and was now rewarded with a sitting-down job dispensing luncheon tickets. Hitler didn't shift her.

Jimmy used at one time to augment his wage-packet with turns at 'the Met' music hall in the Edgware Road. The Assistant Secretary was a member of the Magicians' Circle who liked to perform conjuring tricks for his friends. Reputedly Jimmy and Mr Aird used to practise tap-dancing together on a table.

Poor Ronny: when in 1968–9 he became President he could not do the conjuring trick of averting the Special General Meeting called by angry members following the cancelled tour to South Africa. His chairing of that heated meeting at Church House, Westminster, must have been for him the most hateful event since those wartime battles in the desert in two of which he was the only survivor of his tank crew.

In terms of dedicated service to MCC – twenty-six years as Assistant Secretary, ten as Secretary, then, after an interval on the Committee, President, followed by thirteen as Trustee, and finally appointed a Life Vice-President, sixty years in all – scarcely a handful can stand comparison. Despite having to deal with vastly more complicated issues than any that disturbed Ronny Aird's Secretaryship, Billy Griffith followed him in the same friendly, clubable tradition.

I see in my mind's eye a rich collection of senior characters sporting the red and yellow MCC tie – or, on the field at out-matches, the similar-hued sash holding up their flannels. Let Captain T. H. Carlton Levick epitomize them, a trim little chap with a clipped moustache, who, it was said, used to turn up at departure platforms and greet teams going on MCC tours, saying, 'Hello, you fellows, I'm your manager.' And, paying all his own expenses, he proceeded to fetch and carry as required, radiating good will and complementing the job of the functionary always provided (except in Australia) by the host country. In this self-elected capacity he went twice to the West Indies and once each to South Africa and Canada. He would turn out at a moment's notice if MCC were short for an out-match, and he is named in the 1937 red book which contains the full scores of all MCC matches that year in the list of 'Gentlemen and Professionals who played in less than three matches'. He was then in his seventieth year, yet during the war he functioned as honorary curator, supervising the dispersal to a safe place of the more valuable pictures and books, and caring for the rest.

From the annual scorebooks I see I contrived to play forty matches for MCC in the 1930s – and even to make more than 1200 runs. Above

me in alphabetical lists was H. D. Swan, who managed matches and minor MCC tours, such as to Yorkshire and the Channel Islands. There is no record of 'Swanny' ever making double figures – one year he averaged 1.14 for seven completed innings. A large man, he was an utter non-bender at mid-on, a bland expression unchanging as the ball whistled past his boots. In short, he was the worst I ever saw. *Wisden* put it kindly and truly in its obituary notice: 'He had no pretensions to being a great cricketer, but his happy disposition made him an acquisition on all grounds. . . .'

Let it not be thought that MCC sides were a joke. The Swans and the Levicks collected otherwise good sides, generally supplemented as necessary by youngsters on the groundstaff – Compton (D. C. S.), for instance, Edrich (W. J.), Robertson (J. D.) and many more who, under the wise direction of the head pro, Archie Fowler, later graduated, some to greatness, and all with a grounding in cricket values. Very few at the end of their Lord's apprenticeship turned out bad eggs. Nor do Don Wilson's revolving flock today.

The only faint smudge on the horizon of memory is of the first MCC dinner I recall, a glittering occasion at the Savoy in celebration of the 150th anniversary. No field-sportsman, I found myself placed between two of the gun-making Purdeys, scarcely a felicitous left and right. If I have given the impression of pre-war Lord's, its members and staff, as a happy family that is just as it seems to me, upwards of half a century on. If there were tensions they have blown away with the years. They were blissful, carefree days indeed.

John Arlott's Who's Who *entry describes him as 'wine and general writer', which is a curious phrase for one of the all-time great cricket writers. Sometime clerk in a mental hospital and detective sergeant, his has been one of the most distinctive voices and pens in cricket at least since he wrote* How to Watch Cricket *in 1949.*

'Oos 'e, then?'

JOHN ARLOTT

Lord's changes, and so do those who go there to play or to watch, not exactly starting from the mewling stage but, in many cases, relatively soon afterwards. First, as a rule, comes the autograph stage, and an abiding memory of that is the good temper of the constantly importuned cricketers. The first touring team in England after the war – the Indians – were not only an attraction but an aspect of life that many boys had never known. No picture remains sharper in the memory of those nostalgic-novelty days than one of Mushtaq Ali, the tall, opening batsman, saying to a bunch of lads who surrounded him at the back of Lord's Pavilion, albums in hand, 'Get in line, then, and I will sign them all.' Soon the boys had most of the Indian team lining up also and they marched past them, pencils at the ready, every player signing for all as fast – or nearly as fast – as they came up.

The next stage is the one which specifies: 'I must sit beside the sight-screen as high up as possible so that I see exactly what the ball is doing.' There are also, nowadays, the amateur photographers; indeed, the seating round the Nursery End sight-screen could be extended upwards to a vast extent to satisfy all those eager for a share of that particular coign of vantage.

For the writer, he had reached the sight-screen stage by the time the war broke out: he returned to the joint delights of membership and a

press card. There are delights, indeed, at Lord's; even, on occasion, a good bottle of claret in the members' dining room.

No other British cricket pavilion offers its members quite such advantages. First of all – and what a fine, unforgettable moment that is – there is the occasion when the gateman first recognizes the new member; and, as a general rule, too, the elderly member who has not been there for years and finds himself remembered. There is a standard of feudalism enjoyed in few other resorts of sport, or other activity. It is better than membership of a London club – which, of course, it is – for other ordinary mortals to see the member receive a touch of the bowler (hat not player) and a friendly, but not, of course, familiar, recognition.

It might be argued, without exaggeration, that the treatment of the press is nowhere better than at Lord's. The lunches, for instance, which once were negligible, have improved considerably – or at least they had on the last occasion that this writer had the pleasant chance to taste them. The last important development there was the howling down of the reporter who sought to reconcile the disagreement about red wine or white by opting for rosé. The cricket press never put up a better or more vehement protest than then.

The member of MCC is not confined to cricket: he may take the exercise of being bowled to in the nets – to a public chorus of 'Oos 'e, then?' – when some minor performer avails himself of that facility; or he may prefer squash or real tennis. Most of those who go to Lord's, though, go to watch cricket, to watch it in what is, in fact, a club and not a stadium. Its capacity is no more than 27,000, though that stretches it, and when it is exceeded, the discomfort suffered by some is the most eloquent tribute to the attraction of the game. Anyone who doubts the eminence of Lord's Cricket Ground should observe the reaction of those – even the most distinguished performers – among the Test players of visiting countries, who regard playing there as something of a peak of distinction.

Let us, though, do as the young cricket enthusiast rarely does, and look inwards on the quite remarkable riches which belong legally to Lord's Cricket Ground but also, in effect, to the entire game of cricket. There probably is a general view of members of MCC as being at least 'hearties'. Some may be, but by no means all. Otherwise Lord's would not house such a superb collection of art and literature of the game. The initial credit for that must go to the Victorian gentleman who eventually emerged as Sir Spencer Ponsonby-Fane and began the great Lord's collection, which bequests by members built up to vast size.

Any cricket researcher knows – or ought to know – that the Lord's Library affords quite superb reference. However, it was not until 1987, when a vast clear-out and sale by auction of 845 items from the Lord's collection – paintings, cartoons, prints, bats, balls, cricket clothing, handkerchiefs, almost all duplicates – produced the prodigious sum of £290,000, that the extent of its riches was publicly appreciated. The sum raised will be used to maintain the standard of works of art and historic landmarks for the benefit not merely of members but, once more, for all cricket.

Of course the collection includes period pictures and prints of famous cricket grounds, but there are also mugs, belts, caps and plates which have close connections with cricket. The portraits are wide-ranging, from Lord himself to Sir Don Bradman, and the exhibits run from the sparrow killed in flight by the Cambridge University bowler, Jahangir Khan, to an illuminated emu's egg. There is a miniature grandfather clock made from a beam in the cottage of David Harris, the great Hambledon bowler of the eighteenth century. There is an oil of cricket being played in the Valley of Peace, Christchurch, New Zealand, painted by the great Australian googly bowler, Arthur Mailey; and the Coalport dinner plate issued to celebrate Colin Cowdrey's century of centuries. There is a huge, colourful oil by Henry Garland called *The Winner of the Match*, and another by William Bowyer of the bicentenary match at Lord's in 1987. One pauses, too, over an utter period piece depicting the founders of I Zingari, one of them in mittens and an invalid chair, all three in top hats, and one might be inclined to dismiss it as unimportant but that an anonymous poem about the three subjects contains the lines:

> He who (why I can't explain)
> To honoured name of Ponsonby has added Fane.

Of course, this is a private club and Lord's Pavilion, where so many of these items are displayed, is a private clubhouse. However, except on Test match days, high days and holidays, a member of MCC may introduce a guest to enjoy the gems of the collection. Also, for instance, the Ashes urn itself is in the Memorial Gallery, to which any member of the public has access. The visitor, too, may see the two cricket balls bearing silver plaques inscribed to identify them as those used by Jim Laker on the occasion when he took 19 Australian wickets for 90 runs in the 1956 Test match at Old Trafford. All the while the international nature of the game is emphasized by the bat of Victor Trumper, an Aboriginal nulla-nulla, a Royal Copenhagen porcelain bowl, and a mighty – 36 in high – trophy, about one thousand times the volume of the Ashes urn, presented by J. R. Jayawardena, President of Sri Lanka, for competition between that country and England.

For the average collector, all these items arouse immense covetousness, yet their range is so great that it is difficult for one person to take it all in, even in several visits. Therefore, it is best, where possible, for the visitor to go on a non-playing day when, although this may seem ironic, there is no cricket to distract him from art.

When your team has been beaten part way through the day it is pleasant to think that Lord's will offer you food, drink, and countless distractions to cram interest into what could otherwise be blank time. There have, of course, been moments of aberration, but Lord's is essentially a civilized place, as befits the world's greatest cricket ground – not the biggest, only the greatest.

Brian Johnston, an old friend and contemporary of our opening poet, William Douglas-Home, is as distinctive a voice, though in a different timbre, as John Arlott. He was BBC cricket correspondent from 1963 to 1972 and is a regular member of the radio commentating team, where a weakness for cake in all its forms conceals a formidable knowledge of the game.

Swanton for Pope

BRIAN JOHNSTON

When we got married in 1948 my wife, Pauline, asked me where I wanted to live. 'As near to Lord's as possible,' I replied. I must say she didn't do too badly. Within a few months we were installed in a house in Cavendish Avenue – about 85 yards from the Nursery End of Lord's. It was from here that whenever I went to have a net at Lord's I would walk down the road already padded up with bat in hand – much to the surprise of the locals.

Forty-two years later we are still in St John's Wood, though not so close to Lord's. To walk from Cavendish Avenue it took me 2 minutes, from Hamilton Terrace 8½ minutes, and now from Boundary Road 16 minutes on a good day (I'm older and it's further).

So Lord's has been a very special part of my life – almost a second home. Not just in the summer when, apart from commentating on Tests and other big matches, I often slip in for an hour or two to watch whatever cricket is going on, sitting in the sunshine in the Mound or Grandstand; but in the winter I also go there to visit the Library or the shop, or to the cricket school where I can try to spot the stars of the future.

I first heard of Lord's when I realized that it was the ground on which my boyhood hero, Patsy Hendren, played. I didn't go there until 1926 for my first Eton and Harrow match. It was a great social occasion in those days, with crowds of up to 10,000 parading round the ground during the intervals. All the men and boys were in top hats and tails, sporting carnations or cornflowers. The ladies showed off their new hats and dresses, and much entertaining took place on the various coaches encircling the ground.

I soon collected a coterie of friends who met every year in the 'free' seats at the top of Block G – on the right of the sight-screen. I'm afraid we made an awful noise barracking or shouting support for our particular school. On one occasion a messenger came over from the Pavilion on behalf of Plum Warner, asking 'the young gentlemen' to make less noise. I was later told that due to my misbehaviour, which went on right up until 1939, my election to MCC during the war was put back a year or two.

It was all harmless fun and we had regular visitors such as Frank Mann and two sons, and old Harrovian, Gerald Du Maurier, who came to hear our dreadful jokes. For instance, if a well-dressed, pompous-looking man arrived we would shout out: 'There's a message here from Moss Bros. They say can you return your morning suit to them by six o'clock tonight, as it's needed for a wedding in the morning.' Or, even worse, we would sit behind someone and pin their tails to the seat with drawing pins so that they couldn't get up. All this went on for almost ten years or so after the war and we even had a Block G Eton *v* Harrow match at Hurlingham each summer.

Alas, as a wicket-keeper I never got my XI at Eton so never played in the Lord's match. But in my last year, as compensation, I was allowed into the hallowed Pavilion and spent most of the match in the Eton dressing room eating the cherries which Lord Harris always sent in a large basket every year. I was also given my first tour of Lord's by our coach, George Hirst, a lovely man with a twinkle in his eye and a kind heart. We even went up to the scorer's box over the Grandstand scoreboard, something I have never done again.

Apart from the Eton and Harrow matches I also attended the Easter Classes from 1927 to 1930. I was coached in wicket-keeping by Fred Price of Middlesex and England. In 1937 he caught seven catches in one innings against Yorkshire at Lord's! He was having a drink in the Tavern afterwards when an excited lady rushed up to him and said, 'Oh, Mr Price, when you held your seventh catch I was so thrilled that I nearly fell over the balcony.' 'Well, madam,' replied Fred, 'on my form today I would probably have caught you too.'

Things were different in those days, compared to the marvellous facilities available today. When it rained we had to practise on matting pitches under the Grand and Mound Stands, and the schoolmaster who ran the classes on behalf of MCC was dressed in a blue pin-stripe suit and wore a bowler hat.

I shall always remember Tuesday 1 July 1930. It was the fourth and last day of the Second Test *v* Australia and some of us were allowed up to Lord's for lunch in one of the Tavern boxes. That afternoon we watched Percy Chapman and Gubby Allen attacking the Australian bowling, with Chapman making 121, including four giant sixes off Clarrie Grimmett. Chapman was eventually caught out behind the stumps by Bertie Oldfield. He told our cricket master that he only got out because he had 'a bloody big bluebottle in my eye'! Australia needed 72 to win and there was some excitement when they lost 3 wickets for 22, including – much to our disappointment – Don Bradman, who was brilliantly caught by Chapman low down in the gully. He only made 1, but at least we had caught a glimpse of this magical figure in the baggy green cap.

Except for the Varsity Match each year I saw little cricket at Lord's at that time, but I was lucky enough to see an eighteen-year-old called Compton make a brilliant 87 against Northamptonshire in only his second match for Middlesex. I also saw him play a match-saving 76 not out against Australia in England's second innings of the 1938 Test. And I was privileged to see Wally Hammond's 240 in the first innings, one of the greatest Test innings I ever saw. He slaughtered poor Fleetwood-Smith with some merciless driving.

The next year, 1939, provided a sensation in the Eton and Harrow match. Harrow won for the first time since 1908! Those Etonians present thought it was an unhappy omen, and that it meant war was now inevitable. How right we were!

I paid my next visit to Lord's in 1946 when I did my first television Test commentary against India. Later that year Ronnie Aird kindly asked me to become a member of the Cross Arrows, who in those days played their September matches on the main ground. I played for them twice and had the thrill of changing in the Middlesex dressing room, walking for the first time through the famous Long Room, and out on to the field through the little white gate – a path trodden by countless great cricketers of the past.

In one of the matches played on the edge of the square by the Grandstand, I kept wicket to a chirpy sixteen-year-old off-spinner from Kentish Town. I remember that he had very long hair and that Plum Warner told him to get it cut! Imagine that happening today! It was my first introduction to Freddie Titmus and I have always been proud that I actually made a leg-side stumping off him.

Since then Lord's has played a big part in my commentating career, with county matches, cup finals and Test matches both on television and radio. At the start we had to sit out in the open on the small balcony outside the Committee dining room. We had no cover and used the stone parapet as our table. We often got very wet, with dear old Roy Webber's scoresheets becoming unreadable after being spattered by rain. When the Warner Stand was built both television and radio were moved into boxes there. Radio has since moved back to the Pavilion into our own spacious box on the top balcony above the visitors' dressing room, where we have a superb view of the ground.

This is not a chronicle of Test matches at Lord's but undoubtedly the most exciting one was in 1963 against the West Indies, when Colin Cowdrey emerged with his broken left arm in plaster to join David Allen with 9 wickets down, two balls to go, and 6 runs needed for victory. With Wes Hall bowling at his fastest in poor light, David successfully played the two balls and it was an honourable draw. Colin, a left-hander, did not have to bat, but had he had to do so he intended to bat with his *right* hand.

This exciting finish produced a unique television occasion. The last over was due to start just before six o'clock, and we were ordered to leave Lord's and hand back to Alexandra Palace for the BBC News. It was a terrible thing to have to do and we were all furious and frustrated. But luckily the controller of television was then Kenneth Adam, who was a mad-keen cricketer. He was, of course, viewing and was equally horrified at what had happened. Television was about to miss what could be one of the most exciting Test match finishes ever, and he immediately rang the news-room and told them to go back to Lord's *at once*. The poor news-reader had just begun to read some item about President Kennedy when he received his instructions in his ear-plug. He

stopped in his tracks and hastily said, 'We are now going straight back
to Lord's', just in time for what I think was the second ball of the last
over.

At the beginning of this match Jim Swanton and I were commentators and we were told that they were electing a new Pope in Rome.
Thousands of people were assembled in St Peter's Square awaiting the
white puff of smoke which always comes from the Vatican chimney to
announce that a new Pope *has* been elected. We were advised that as
soon as this happened BBC-TV would immediately leave London and
go straight over to Rome to find out who the new Pope was. As I
commentated I was waiting for this call to Rome when I suddenly
noticed that the old Tavern chimney had caught fire and black smoke
was belching out. We immediately switched our cameras on to it, and I
was able to say, 'There you are. Jim Swanton has been elected Pope!'
He was delighted!

We always tried to have fun with our cameras and on one occasion I
spotted J. J. Warr sitting in the Grandstand with his fiancée, Valerie. I
couldn't resist saying, 'Warr and Piece'.

Another time was when the Lord's Taverners were playing an Old
England XI one Sunday. Our cameras were showing Norman Wisdom
playing the fool as he batted, falling about all over the place, and caus-
ing tremendous laughter among the large crowd. An MCC member
had fallen asleep but suddenly woke up and saw Norman's antics.
After a few seconds he turned to his neighbour and said, 'I don't know
how good a cricketer that chap is, but he'd make a bloody fine
comedian.'

I've only made one of my many gaffes at Lord's. It happened in 1969
when Alan Ward, playing in his first Test, was bowling very fast from
the Pavilion End to Glenn Turner, of New Zealand. Off the fifth ball of
one of his overs Glenn was struck a terrible blow in the box. He collapsed in the crease, writhing in pain. The camera panned in on him and I
had to waffle away as he lay there. After about 2 minutes he slowly got
up. I reported: 'Someone is handing him his bat, and although he looks
rather pale and shaky, he's pluckily going to continue batting. One ball
left!'

In May 1987 I decided, after fifteen years and 732 programmes, to
give up my BBC radio programme 'Down Your Way'. I was given the
choice of where I wanted to go for my last broadcast and I without

hesitation chose Lord's. MCC did me proud and it was one of the happiest days of my life. On arrival I noticed that the Grandstand scoreboard had put up a total of 733, the highest score ever recorded on it. The previous highest had been 729 made by Australia in 1930. At that time they had no figure 7 and had to hang out a tin number plate with 7 on it in front of the 29.

I always interviewed six people on the programme and my 'victims' at Lord's that day included the President, Colin Cowdrey; the Secretary, Lt Col. John Stephenson; the curator, Stephen Green; the groundsman, Mick Hunt; and Nancy Doyle, who has presided over the best table on the county circuit for twenty-eight years. In addition to looking after all the players and officials, she caters for the Committee's lunches and for the more modest needs of our commentary box. Each morning during a match we get coffee and biscuits, with a special packet of two brown-bread meat sandwiches for me. For the sixth 'victim' to represent all the great players who had played at Lord's, I chose Denis Compton. So it was a fair representation of all that Lord's means.

MCC gave a lunch in honour of the programme and presented me with an MCC mug. It was a perfect day with only one slight snag. Both the President and Denis chose 'My Way' for their piece of music. But Colin kindly gave way and selected 'Underneath the Arches', which, by coincidence, is the only tune I can now play on the piano.

In the summer of 1989 – sixty-three years after my first visit in 1926 – I commentated on my fifty-second Test at Lord's, far more than at any other ground. During these years I have made so many friends at Lord's – the Secretariat, the players, the Pavilion attendants, the gatemen and the groundstaff. They have always made me welcome. Imagine, therefore, my delight when towards the end of the summer I received a letter from the President, Field Marshal Lord Bramall, saying that I had been elected by the Committee to be an honorary life member of Lord's.

My cup overflowed at such an honour. You can understand, perhaps, why I feel justified in calling it 'My Lord's'.

Marble and Bronze

JOHN WOODCOCK

The Lord's Test match has been called the command performance of the English cricket season, and when Neville Cardus was in attendance he was a celebrated part of it. Either in front of the old Tavern, or in the Long Room, or on the coach mound behind what is now the Warner Stand and was then a low enclosure, he would hold court, talking, as he once said of C. B. Fry, 'for art's sake'.

To be sure that he had your eye as well as your ear, Neville would stand, if you were alone, immediately in front of you with his back to the cricket, prodding you in the shoulder if your attention seemed to be straying towards the play. When he laughed, which he did a lot for he had a great sense of fun, he would throw back his head and put his hand to his mouth.

In Adelaide, towards the end of the MCC tour of 1950–1, he gave me a copy of *Second Innings*, the follow-up to his *Autobiography*, and inscribed it: 'To John Woodcock. In friendship and with apologies for verbal abuse addressed at him, all of it entirely justifiable.' So when, in 1952, I reported my first Lord's Test match, for the *Manchester Guardian*, there in the Long Room each morning was their most illustrious critic, bearing a copy of the paper and offering words of encouragement. That was a long time ago, but it is still as real as the present minute.

The Lord's press box of those days was the white building to the left of the Pavilion as you look out at the ground. It now houses the MCC

Secretariat. We were upstairs, the groundstaff down below. The difference between the writing of the 1950s and the 1990s is mainly one of emphasis. The press box forty years ago was occupied by more 'cricket writers' and fewer 'journalists'. There was, I think, less 'clever' writing, by which I mean there were fewer writers trying to be clever. If there was greater propriety, that is because it was the way of the world; perhaps there was more cricket wisdom; but there is certainly no less humour today.

In that Lord's Test match of 1952, when Vinoo Mankad produced, for India, an astonishing all-round display, there was not, as far as I remember, a press conference in the members' writing room after the close of play, at which he 'talked us through it'. There were still some years to go before readers began to be informed as much of what the players themselves had thought of the play as of what the writers had. I very much doubt whether Cardus or R. C. Robertson-Glasgow or any of my predecessors on *The Times* ever went to a press conference in their lives, and Jim Swanton would have gone to very few.

Having fallen out with the Indian Cricket Board, Mankad was spending the summer of 1952 in the Lancashire League when he was prevailed upon to play in the last three Tests against England. The hurt of seeing India lose their first four second-innings wickets without a run on the board in the First Test at Headingley may have influenced him. Be that as it may, at Lord's he scored 72 and 184, going in first against an attack that was opened by Bedser and Trueman and had Laker to follow; and with his orthodox left-arm spin he did his best to keep India in the game by returning figures in England's first innings of 73-24-196-5.

England still won easily enough, but by the time they did so, on the fifth morning, Mankad had been on the field for almost the entire match. In over 100 years, no other Lord's Test has seen anything to compare with it as an all-round feat. In the forty-nine which I have written about, Ian Botham probably came nearest to matching it. When Garfield Sobers scored his two big hundreds here, in 1966 and 1973, he did nothing very much with the ball, and when Keith Miller took 10 wickets in the Australian victory of 1956 he left it to the others to make the runs. In 1982 Kapil Dev had a memorable match, scoring 41 and then an explosive 89 in only fifty-five balls, and taking 8

England wickets. Botham's year was 1978, when he beat Pakistan almost single-handed by scoring 108 in England's only innings and taking 8 for 34 in Pakistan's second.

That, though, was when several of Pakistan's best cricketers had been bought up by Mr Packer. Nothing else that I have known to happen at Lord's, not even the most wicked of bouncers, has sent such a shiver down my spine as Packer's pronouncement, made as he and his lieutenants left the Committee Room on 23 June 1977. 'Now it's every man for himself,' he said, 'and let the devil take the hindmost.' He was to change, irrevocably, the face of cricket.

So, by doing all the Indian batting and all the Indian bowling, Mankad made a good story to start one off at Lord's, and not many years pass without a *tour de force* from someone. It is hardly possible to arrive at the ground too early on the morning of a Test match. There is nowhere else like it for meeting friends, and for watching the players practise or getting the feel of a great sporting occasion. The green bank where Cardus stood no longer provides a view of the play, but it is still a favourite vantage point for watching the world go by.

Here, from the direction of the Pavilion, come Ted Dexter, whose innings of marble and bronze against West Indies in 1963 remains such a vivid memory, and Colin Milburn, whose hooking of the Australians in 1968 brought the crowd to its feet. Here, too, are Keith Miller, in England for Royal Lord's and Royal Ascot, and Richie Benaud, as immaculately groomed as on the day he held that blinding catch in the gully to send back Colin Cowdrey and in the same match made a dazzling 97. And over there is Cowdrey himself, leaning slightly forward as he shares a joke with Everton de Courcy Weekes, whose 90 on a nasty pitch in 1957 prompted Ronny Aird, then Secretary of MCC, to despatch to the West Indian dressing room a note, written in his own hand and on the members' behalf, congratulating him on his conspicuously brave and marvellously resourceful batting. Weekes must be in England to represent Barbados at bridge, the game at which he now excels. But there goes the five-minute bell and it is time to take one's seat. It is all a part of the pageant of Lord's.

So, in a different way, was the mother of one of the Cambridge side, some time in the 1970s. It was a Saturday-Monday-Tuesday University Match, and on the Saturday it was my turn to come up with a sporting feature for the centre pages. I attempted something evocative on university cricket, hoping that it might give the match a small but much needed boost.

Well, on the Monday morning, after parking my car behind the real tennis court, I ran into this light blue parent, or perhaps I should say she ran into me. I saw her coming, all disarmingly. 'We read your piece in Saturday's *Times*,' she said, 'and decided it wasn't one for the scrapbook.' How the great Cardus laughed when, soon afterwards, I found him in the Long Room and told him. Back went his head with joy, and then, as though remembering he was in a holy place, his hand came up to his mouth, as if to stifle such impiety!

After that fearsome foursome a little literary light relief. Philip Howard, sometime fast bowler and swashbuckling six-hitter for the Eton Ramblers and a variety of writerish occasional XIs, is well known for his articles on words. These are some of the very few things still worth reading in The Times, *so here he offers some lordly thoughts on lexicography.*

Lord's and the Language

PHILIP HOWARD

Lord's has left its mark on the national lexicon as well as on the national character. The eponym himself, Thomas Lord (1755–1832), was more successful as nomenclator and property developer than he was as cricketer. He does not even make it into *The Dictionary of National Biography*. The only Thomas Lord to get into that national Valhalla is a now forgotten bird-man who between 1791 and 1796 published a serial work entitled *Lord's Entire New System of Ornithology, or Oecumenical History of British Birds*. But the cricketing Thomas Lord achieved the much rarer distinction of becoming a national byword and having his name recorded at length in *The Oxford English Dictionary*.

He was lucky with his name, so apt for the proverbial English love of a lord. Just as the horse race is called the Derby rather than the Bunbury only because of the toss of a coin, the cricket ground might just as well have been called after one of Lord's collaborating founding fathers – the Earl of Winchilsea and Charles Lennox, later the Duke of Richmond. Earl's or Duke's would not have been so simply snobbish; Winchilsea's or Lennox's are hard to say because of the sibilants; Richmond's would have been geographically confusing, bringing to mind the south-west suburb, which in any case gets its name from a Yorkshire town that was part of the title of the Welsh usurper, Henry VII.

The first reference to Lord's that I can find in the infant *Times* (the cataloguing and design of these early issues are incoherent) is on 3/4 June 1799, fourteen years after the foundation of the paper and twelve years after the foundation of that other national institution: 'The colours were presented to the corps in Lord's cricket-ground.' In the year that Napoleon was winning battles across Europe and establishing himself as first consul of France, the English were thinking of bloodier sports than cricket. The ground mentioned was the original one, where Dorset Square now stands. The *Times* reference indicates that the name Lord's was already well enough known to its largely metropolitan readership to be dropped in without editorial gloss.

Within a few summers the ground had moved twice, further west each time, to finish at its present site, and was established in the national idiolect. For example, here is Arthur Munby, the diarist and poet who nourished a secret obsession for Victorian working women, on 10 July 1863: 'Miss Williams had asked me to go with her party to the Eton and Harrow cricket match at Lord's.'

As the century progressed, memory faded of the founding father, the not very good Yorkshire cricketer Thomas Lord, who was briefly on the staff of the Old White Conduit Club, and people started to refer to the ground solecistically, without the apostrophe, as Lords. Here is *Blackwood's Magazine* from 1910: 'The Australians had won the toss at Lords. . . . Our visitors had already on a Lords wicket pretty thoroughly extended an MCC eleven.' And here is an example of the solecism from an Australian book published in 1972: 'When there's a Test on at Lords, radio stations cater to the thousands who sit up till dawn.'

A certain snobbery has always been part of cricket. People started to suppose that Lord's referred to peers generally rather than the founder. In any case, the English are as careless with their apostrophes as they are with their slip catches, as you can see in any greengrocer's with his apple's and pear's. The worst I saw was at a stall in Oxford Street at the time of the wedding of the Prince and Princess of Wales, which advertised for sale in capitals: ROYAL PENIS. What it had in mind was Royal Pen's. Lord's is etymologically correct, and preserves the history of the ground in punctuation. But Lords is also widely used, and is accordingly also part of the language; as such it is recorded by *The Oxford English Dictionary*, which is there to record English as it is used rather than to pronounce on correctitude. Perhaps we should simplify life by abolishing the apostrophe.

The Pavilion has been part of Lord's since the beginning. Here is a continuation of that original extract from *The Times* of 1799, about the ground being used to present colours to the troops: 'After the military ceremony was over, the Earl and Countess partook of a cold collation provided for them in the pavillion [*sic*].' Women, or at any rate countesses, were allowed into the Pavilion in those primitive days. But this was not the stately red-brick pleasure dome we know and love, but a tent or marquee. The name 'pavilion' comes from *papilio*, the Latin for a butterfly, because its fluttering canvas was compared to a butterfly's wings. An example of English suet-pudding humour, except that the Old French made the joke first, and we cribbed it from them.

Our present Pavilion was accepted as part of the language almost as soon as it was erected. Here is W. G. Grace in his book called *Cricket*, published in 1891: 'The handsome Pavilion which was recently built at Lord's. . . . It is capable of accommodating 3000 people.' Rather more than that these days, sir, all wearing their silly ties in colours that no gaudy butterfly, not even in the Amazon rainforest, would be seen dead in.

By contrast, the Nursery End is a recent arrival into the national vocabulary. The earliest reference to it that the Oxford lexicographers could find (and they are notoriously difficult to pre-date) was in a book by Walter Hammond called *Cricketers' School*, published in 1950: 'Yorkshire does not run the usual cricket Nursery that a team like Middlesex maintains.' Note the elegant variation: Wally was more at home with his on-drives than his prose. Nursery had been in the language as a wet joke for an establishment for training young players for three centuries before it arrived at Lord's. But the players were actors. Here is Pepys on 2 August 1664: 'Tom Killigrew is setting up a nursery; that is, is going to build a house in Moorefields, wherein he will have common plays acted.' The gloss that Pepys felt necessary to add in his diary, in cipher and intended for his eyes only, indicates that this metaphorical use of nursery was unfamiliar and therefore, for Pepys was a logophile and a good journalist, new.

We should not be surprised that the Tavern is by far the oldest of the names of Lord's that have established themselves in the language. It comes from the Latin *trabs*, a tree-trunk, beam, or plank, with the suffix *-erna* as found in 'cavern' and 'cistern'. Writers as judicious as Cicero and Tacitus used *taverna*, a shed constructed of boards, to mean an inn or boozer. The word came into English as early as 1286, with a critical reference to the contemporary lager louts in the royal rolls of Edward I. Shakespeare had prophetic knowledge of the lifestyle of the Lord's Taverners, as revealed in *Richard II*, V. iii. 5: 'Can no man tell of my unthrifty Sonne? Enquire at London, 'mongst the Tavernes there.' Once Lord's had opened, literature is thick with references to the institution: 'The Taverns are the Nurseries of Profaneness and Treason.' This author has got his ends mixed up, but he has the message about the Tavern. And here is Dickens in Chapter 2 of *Barnaby Rudge*: 'This Tavern would seem to be a house of call for all the gaping idlers of the neighbourhood.'

The nomenclature of Lord's and the vocabulary of cricket form a significant part of the English language. Because of the Packer revolution and other deplorable changes in the game, many of the terms of cricketing jargon have changed their meanings substantially. Cricket is one of the fields most in need for revision in the *OED*, along with Victorian scientific and medical terminology. The lexicographers are turning their attention to it now. But while English is spoken, Lord's and the Pavilion, the Nursery and the Tavern are part of it.

While on the subject of words this seems the correct spot for Stephen Green, MCC's Curator, a man who already appears to be as much a fixture as the Old Father Time weather vane. His Library, incidentally, is a mine of information and a very agreeable place in which to work. Green himself is well set, I should say, to becoming an institution in his own right.

Lord's from the Library

STEPHEN GREEN

'Of course if you take that position as curator of MCC you may have great difficulty in ever leaving it.' So spoke Mr Patrick King, the wise and kindly county archivist of Northamptonshire, to his youngest and most impetuous colleague in the spring of 1968.

Twenty-two years later, probably unemployable anywhere else, I have often pondered the wisdom of these words. But why should I want to leave Lord's?

My feelings for the place alternate between the lofty sentiments of Sir Robert Menzies that the Long Room is the Cathedral of Cricket and the words of an anonymous wit that Lord's is the only lunatic asylum run by its inmates! As usual, the truth seems to lie somewhere between the two.

Most days start with the opening of the post. Even the outside of the envelope can spring some surprises. In the week that Cardinal Hume was elected a member of MCC I received a letter from Trinidad addressed to Lourdes Cricket Ground. Other odd addresses have included Maryland Cricket Club and Lord's Ground, London, Ontario. The most unusual envelope, however, came in 1973. It was addressed to Dr W. G. Grace. When I pointed out that the member in question had died in 1915 my correspondent replied that he was distressed to learn of the death of his dear cousin.

The contents of the letters are just as varied. Correspondents from the Indian sub-continent are quite likely to give one a premature knighthood! Students want information on such esoteric subjects as the ergonomics of cricket, whilst Australians frequently imagine that a curator is an expert on such matters as manure and fertilizers rather than museum and library topics. MCC receives so many letters from French schoolchildren that we have prepared a leaflet on 'Le jeu de cricket'.

Once the post has been read, the telephone calls start. During the postal strike of 1971 the girl on the switchboard, fresh from school and flustered by the enormous number of incoming calls, announced: 'I shall put you through to Mr Green, our creator.' There was also a lady librarian who could only with difficulty be convinced that a certain well-known cricket writer was not named Harlot.

After the phone calls there are people to be shown around. These come from all parts of the cricket-playing world and sometimes from countries not normally associated with the game. There are many school parties. I well remember the day when the master in charge arrived 5 minutes before his pupils to warn me that during his twenty-five years at this particular school he had taught seven convicted murderers, not including the Kray twins whose case was at the time sub judice!

Australian tourists are prone sooner or later to say during the tour, 'Now I should like to see The Oval, please.' One needs to resist the temptation to recommend a trip to South London on the 159 bus from St John's Wood. They only want to see the square.

It is difficult to help some visitors. One gentleman arrived whose knowledge of English seemed to be non-existent. I eventually produced an atlas to see if he could show his country of origin. He firmly pointed to the middle of Rumania. I think he had confused Lord's with the Zoological Gardens.

On another occasion forty bishops and their wives came to Lord's during a break in the 1988 Lambeth Conference. When I asked my vicar if he ever addressed forty bishops, he replied, 'No, thank God.'

Some years ago a beauty queen from down under wanted to take back a piece of the Lord's turf. Jim Fairbrother, the then head groundsman, readily obliged but, alas, the Australian authorities would not allow her to take it into the country.

Quite a lot of the day is, of course, spent in trying to help the members of MCC. I well remember the time in 1970 when there had been a minor but distressing burglary on the ground. Police enquiries were proceeding vigorously and I came back to the office feeling tired and depressed. I had lost a small but treasured possession. Back in the Library I encountered a sweet old member who beamed on me and said, 'What I like about Lord's is that it is such a peaceful place.'

One is privileged to get to know many distinguished members. As an undergraduate at Brasenose College, Oxford, I did not often encounter the august personage of the vice-chancellor of the university. At Lord's, however, I have been lucky enough to enjoy the company of two eminent holders of that high office, Sir John Masterman and Sir Walter Oakeshott.

And then, of course, there are the players. They normally come across my bows only when the weather is bad or when they have retired, but some current cricketers do take a lively interest in cricket's artistic and literary heritage. This can lead to complications. I once infelicitously referred to the beautiful spouse of a well-known cricketer as his 'ex model wife'.

There are sometimes dealings with the press and the media. Some interviews go better than others. On one occasion I'm afraid I said, 'I think if there were a fire at Lord's the first thing I would grab would be the Ashes.'

Many schoolboys think that the famous urn contains the ashes of W. G.'s beard. Others allege that inside it are the remains of an Aboriginal cricketer who died in England during the 1868 tour. The loan of the Ashes to Australia in 1988 certainly caused many problems, not least the imponderable difficulties of insuring such a unique and celebrated object.

I have played at Lord's but only on the Nursery and only in a staff match. When I was bowled by one of my lady colleagues I decided it was time to retire.

MCC's curator receives countless invitations to speak about Lord's. These have taken me to the American Embassy, to New Scotland Yard, to London Zoo, to an almshouse designed by Sir Christopher Wren, to Oxford and Cambridge colleges, to a hotel down under in Perth, to a university in Philadelphia, and to many venues up and down Britain.

Just occasionally there is time to do some research for publication about Lord's and the great figures in its history. With the late Jim Coldham, for example, I was able to explore in the India Office Library the papers of the great MCC figure, Lord Harris. These related to his governorship of Bombay in Victorian times. It was moving to read the words of Lord Harris: 'My heart is with the dwellers in the country villages, who are prey to ignorance, sickness and solitude: and whom I want to help if I can. . . .' Lord Harris was one of the greatest men ever to have worn an MCC tie.

Sometimes one is able to acquire fresh treasures for the Club. In my time at Lord's we have obtained, for example, a complete cricket outfit dating from *c*. 1820; the portrait of C. B. Fry by Edmund Nelson; the watercolour drawing by Felix of the All England XI; Thomas Lord's punchbowl; and John Ward's portrait and Neale Andrew's bust of Sir George Allen. Perhaps the acquisition which gave me the greatest thrill was the purchase of the portrait by Nathaniel Dance of Thomas Lord's patron, George, Earl of Winchilsea. Sir Pelham Warner described the sitter as 'the founder of the MCC'. Its purchase was a splendid vindication of the policy of holding a sale in order to benefit the Club's Museum and Library.

Mention of Lord Winchilsea reminds us that Lord's has been an integral part of the national scene since the year the first fleet set sail for Australia. It was in existence before the Bastille was stormed. MCC formulated the rules for lawn tennis when Wimbledon was only a croquet club. There are days when Lord's is the hub of the country and it is a great privilege to serve it in a small capacity.

Finally, the curator always gets the last word: he writes the obituary notices in the MCC Annual Report.

Lord Deedes, of course, became an institution years ago, first as a Member of Parliament – a cabinet minister, no less – and then as Editor of The Daily Telegraph. *There is no more sagacious journalist writing – on cricket, politics, or life itself. If, as I slightly fear, Stephen Green were to run himself out early on, any partnership between Philip Howard and Deedes would be hugely entertaining.*

Grandmother's Footsteps

W. F. DEEDES

My early recollections of Lord's were heavily influenced by my grandmother. She was a strong-minded woman, bless her, very much in charge of family affairs until she died in her nineties. When I first came to London to work in the early 1930s and lived in her house, she instructed me to go to Huntsman for my suits, to Peal for my shoes, and to become a member of the MCC.

And as to that, she added, there would be no difficulty. My uncle (who lived in the same house) never went to Lord's. My grandmother had written to the Secretary of the MCC – an old family friend – instructing him to transfer my uncle's membership to me. The letter from Lord's, politely informing my grandmother that this proposed arrangement was out of the question, opened a long, and for me increasingly embarrassing, correspondence.

I developed a nervous apprehension about approaching the ground. Very likely, I reasoned, they had been warned about me at the gates: 'Watch out for a young fellow named Deedes, whose grandmother is trying to sneak him in through the back door.' Once or twice I approached the turnstiles at the Nursery End, which seemed furthest away from the main business of Lord's and so safer. When passing behind the Pavilion I moved circumspectly; they would know all about me in there. A trying time, adolescence.

Nor were my earliest recollections of Lord's much happier. For boys

57

at Eton or Harrow in those days the Lord's match in July was an elaborate and serious ritual. 'What kind of a waistcoat are you thinking of?' a contemporary asked me early in my first summer term. The thought had not entered my head. 'A special waistcoat – and a cane – are essential,' he asserted confidently. So it proved to be. I invested in a grey water-silk waistcoat at the school tailor; goodness knows what it cost my parents. The cane with its round silver knob and dark blue tassle was used, I think, on no other occasion.

In those days attendance at Lord's for the two days of the match was obligatory. Those who turned the break into a long weekend at home were considered to be outside the pale. After stumps were drawn on the first day, it was essential to be seen at a good theatre. The whole thing assumed nightmare proportions in my mind. Two maiden aunts and an uncle, who lived in London, came to the rescue and turned the whole affair into a beano. After dark they took me to see Evelyn Laye in *Blue Eyes*.

In those days there was an enormous attendance at Lord's for this match. Much of fashionable London in Ascot raiment paraded round the ground. The smartest families hired coaches, which stood on the edge of the ground between the Pavilion and the old Tavern. From these they consumed ample lunches from hampers. There were a lot of rich Harrovians in my day, whose fathers had made pots of money in the First World War.

At my second Lord's a year later I spotted an Old Harrovian I faintly knew wearing a blue suit. He had been a tremendous blood at the school during my first two terms and had since left. I remember marvelling at the nerve of someone who was prepared to face the crowd at Lord's in a blue suit. He would go far, I reasoned. He finished up by running a nightclub.

We look back now, those of us who can remember, on those days at Lord's as symbolic of a social order we are happier without. They were nothing of the kind. The Varsity Match, Eton *v* Harrow and, I dare add, Gentlemen *v* Players, to say nothing of Lord's Schools *v* The Rest, enhanced the wonderful variety of cricket to be seen at Lord's.

I look back on the Lord's of that period as a theatre on the stage of which all sorts of players were called upon to perform. I have known in my life a number of men who acquitted themselves well in the Lord's match, playing for Eton or Harrow. Through my eyes it left on them a singular badge of distinction. The last time I went to the Eton and Harrow match was in the summer of 1939. I fell in with a young friend and neighbour, just down from Eton, and we spent a happy afternoon together. A year later, aged nineteen, he was killed in the battle for France.

It took me some time after the war to pick up the threads at Lord's again. I missed it altogether in 1946, while occupied in resettling myself. I caught glimpses, but no more, of Compton and Edrich there in 1947. Not until I had been in Parliament a year or two did there open for me, in unusual circumstances, the most enjoyable chapter of my life at Lord's.

One of my earliest friends in the Commons was Christopher Hollis, then MP for Devizes. He was a devout supporter of Somerset, I was a Man of Kent; but this did not seriously interfere with the arrangements we made. If the House sat all night, and if Somerset, Kent, or anyone else sufficiently interesting were playing at Lord's, we spent the next day there.

In the summers of those days long parliamentary sittings were frequent. How delicious it was to arrive in a taxi soon after eleven at Lord's and there, drowsily, to sit in the sun, watch the play and discuss the mysteries of life. The most delicious moment of all would come after lunch, at about three o'clock. 'You know,' Christopher Hollis would say in his corncrake voice, 'the whips are expecting us back at four o'clock.'

'They want us back at four o'clock? I think we are very comfortable where we are.' That was the magic hour. Somebody usually made a hundred or took a lot of unexpected wickets. I look back on the hours stolen from the government whips at Lord's as the best-spent hours of my life. The next day we would awake deeply refreshed.

There were other experiences there. As a young reporter, working from this country on the 'Bodyline' controversy of 1932-3, I faintly remember visits to Lord's to cover the comings and goings of senior figures. It struck me then and remains with me now that the further politicians distance themselves from the Long Room, the better for the game.

I remember a very long, hot Saturday under the Mound Stand in 1930, accompanied by my uncle, where we watched Bradman and Woodfull assist Australia to a total of 729 for 6. Percy Chapman was the England captain that year; and I do not recall that any of the newspapers called for his head. Those who were watching – from the press box as well as the Pavilion at Lord's – were more discerning than we are today. They knew when we were facing a better side, and how to acknowledge it more gracefully than we do now.

I thought of all these days in the early summer of 1989, when they were kind enough to invite me to Lord's to propose at their annual dinner the toast to Cricket, the MCC and the Australians. 'Are you nervous?' a friend asked, while we were taking a drink in the Tavern before dinner. No, I was not nervous. Sitting between the President and his newly appointed successor, and looking about me at Allan Border's team and the MCC members assembled, I said consolingly to myself: 'There is not a soul here who can possibly know about my grandmother.'

The next author may not be a literary lion but like Lord Deedes he has a formidable reputation as an after-dinner speaker. He is also the first contributor to venture a cavil about that legendary figure, MCC Gateman. I, personally, have a sneaking regard for this man, but if anyone is going to have a go at him then no one is better qualified than J. J. Warr, a former MCC President who took more than seven hundred wickets in his career with Middlesex.

'A Woman!...
Talking to Swanton!'

J. J. WARR

A walled garden with a well-kept lawn, a shrine, a St John's Wood version of Fort Knox, a potential building site, a rest-home for retired colonels, a museum with indifferent catering, or even the Vatican of cricket; many views have been expressed over the years on the status of Lord's. I prefer to see it as the supreme theatre of the game where the strutters and fretters have served up great drama with the odd comedy thrown in. But much of the humour has gone on backstage, unheralded and unsung by the many thousands sitting in the auditorium.

We move to August 1954 with Frank Tyson bowling for Northamptonshire versus Middlesex. He knows the selectors are watching for candidates for the forthcoming tour to Australia and he is trying to 'get on the boat'. His bowling is reaching the speed of the modern Exocet. Bill Edrich, possibly one of the best hookers the game has known, has gone for one hook too many and, beaten for speed, the ball has crashed into his face just below the cheekbone. There is blood everywhere and a stretcher is summoned. Bill is carried into the dressing room and a doctor is piped for over the Pavilion tannoy. We wait anxiously to see if the Hippocratic oath is alive and well. The door

of the dressing room opens and a very elderly white-haired man on sticks, wearing glasses like the bottom of tumblers, feels his way to the massage table where Bill is lying. 'I am a doctor,' he says. 'Where is the patient?' We notice he is looking down at Bill's anatomy rather lower than his bloodstained face. It is pointed out that the injury is facial.

'I shan't be any good in that case,' he says. 'I'm a retired gynaecologist.'

On to 1955 when Statham is bowling the first ball of the South African innings from the Pavilion End to Jackie McGlew. That season there has been much talk of ridges and green wickets at Lord's. The old professionals' room adjoining the writing room to the left of the Pavilion looking out is occupied by old England players specially invited by the MCC. Statham moves in and bowls probably the most lethal opening delivery ever seen in a Test match. It leaps chest height and then cuts away from over the off stump and Godfrey Evans takes a jumping catch 30 yards back with the ball hitting his gloves like a rifle shot. McGlew out first ball and walking back disconsolately to the Pavilion. Frank Woolley is one of those in the old England room, standing on the balcony. He leans forward to get a good view of the ground rather like a Roman emperor about to signal a good breakfast for the lions. 'Statham's bowling without a long-on, I see,' he says, and we realize that the generation gap is not a new phenomenon.

The scene is now the Grace Gates during a recent England–Australia Test match. The visitor at the gate is none other than Sebastian Coe, who has obviously been promised a ticket by one of the players who has forgotten to supply it. The conversation with one of the Lord's gatemen goes as follows. (It must be remembered that most of the gatemen trained under Attila the Hun.)

'Has a ticket for Sebastian Coe been left here by one of the players?'

'I will look, but I don't remember any name like that. No, I am afraid there isn't. But sometimes tickets are left at the North Gate on the other side of the ground.'

'No, he definitely said the Grace Gates. Surely you recognize me as Sebastian Coe?'

'I'm not really up in these things but if you really are Sebastian Coe it shouldn't take you long to run round to the North Gate.'

The scene now shifts to the Committee Room in the Pavilion where Her Majesty the Queen is paying a traditional visit to a Test match. The procedure is that the hierarchy of cricket is introduced to the Queen in a reception line. Then she sits in the window and various individuals are placed next to her for short periods so that she has a chance to talk to as many people as possible. At the end of an over members tend to move about to stretch their legs. One ancient worthy walks by the window, glancing briefly towards the occupants. He rejoins his colleagues in the Long Room.

'I have just seen the most extraordinary thing,' he exclaims. 'There is a woman in the Committee Room talking to Swanton.'

But perhaps my favourite backstage character was Jim Sims. He was a formidable leg-spin bowler but also a good striker of the ball if conditions suited him. In this particular match he had taken 5 wickets in each innings and scored 50 runs in his first knock. I joined him at the crease in the second innings with about 30 runs needed to win and only 2 wickets in hand. I thought a tactical talk was called for so that the old professional could control affairs.

'How shall we play it, Jim?' I asked.

He thought for a moment. 'I don't think it matters a lot, J. J.,' he said, 'because whatever happens I'm covered in bloody glory.'

Forcing the Hand

RACHAEL HEYHOE FLINT

International women's cricket was first seen at Lord's exactly fifty years after the formation of the Women's Cricket Association in 1926. But it was worth the wait! The governing body of women's cricket had applied regularly to the MCC for international matches to be staged there, but the answer was always the same: Lord's wished 'to reduce commitments on the playing square, rather than increase them'.

In 1976 the Australian women's cricket team toured England. To celebrate the Golden Jubilee of the WCA an extra-special plea was made for Lord's to be the venue for one of the three Tests or one-day Internationals. Even when the tour started at the end of May, there was only a faint hope that this would happen. England *might* play at Lord's on Wednesday 4 August, but only if Middlesex (the men) either failed to reach the quarter-final of the (then) Gillette Cup or, if they did reach it, were drawn away.

Praise be to the generosity of Middlesex. They lost to Lancashire by three wickets. This allowed our One-Day game to be moved from the minor surroundings of Sunbury Cricket Club to Lord's, to play for the St Ivel Cream Jug – what a splendidly named trophy! 'Lord's gives in to the Ladies,' said the national press, predictably.

During the build-up to achieving my ambition – to lead England in such a famous Test arena – I unwittingly created situations and antagonism between myself and the WCA officers. A year later, these led to my losing the England captaincy and being sacked from the England team, despite having a Test average against Australia of 87.5. In fact, throughout my twenty-four-year span as an England player and eleven years as captain, I often seemed to antagonize the WCA officers in my efforts to publicize, promote and market women's cricket, so the build-up to playing at Lord's at last was no exception.

Eighteen months in advance of the Australians' 1976 visit I was given a brief by the WCA to promote the event and get sponsorship for it. If we could get a match at Lord's, television coverage and sponsorship would rapidly follow, so in order to try to 'force the hand', I 'popped in' to Lord's towards the end of 1975 to see the MCC Secretary, Jack Bailey. I knew that I had overstepped the bounds of protocol, by bearding the lion in his den, but I am a stubborn, persistent so-and-so and I wanted a commitment. Jack Bailey was polite but no more. He followed up our meeting with a letter expressing the usual platitudes, but offering no hope.

Despairing of getting the right answer from Lord's, I flung myself in at the deep end and floated a story to the national media. I was at a Sports Council reception in London in December 1975 and was talking to Frank Taylor of the *Daily Mirror*. Frank wanted to know if my 'play-at-Lord's-wish' had been granted. I half-jokingly confided that Lord's committees were being obstructive to my ambitions. If they didn't let us play there, I told him, I would report the MCC to the Equal Opportunities Commission!

My tongue-in-cheek story hit the *Daily Mirror* the next day. Radio news programmes and every national paper and agency latched on to my 'threat' and the phone never stopped ringing at home. The WCA were furious at my outburst – but at least we got some magnificent publicity.

We reported to the Lord's nets the day before the match, and as usual I was wearing my Adidas cricket training shoes (which I had bought myself). Seeing them, the WCA vice-chairman rushed over to me, whipped out a tube of shoe whitener and erased the three green stripes on my shoes. It was a Lord's and TCCB ruling at that time that no advertising material was to be exhibited by players.

I also got the blame for two photographs which appeared in the national press. One picture was of our two-year-old son, Ben, and me,

just by the nets after we had finished practising ('not the sort of picture we like to see,' said WCA officials). The other picture was in the *Daily Express* (across six columns) and showed the Australian girls in various stages of undress. They were not allowed to change in the Pavilion on practice day, but were sent to the public ladies' lavatories behind the Mound Stand. Hilaria McCarthy, the ever alert *Daily Express* photographer, nipped into the ladies' cloakroom and captured a brilliant photo.

The England team stayed at the Westmoreland Hotel, at the back of Lord's, on the eve of the match. I was so excited, I hardly slept. I was so nervous I couldn't eat breakfast. To play at Lord's was my life's ambition and I didn't want anything to go wrong on the great day.

I drove myself one-handed to the ground in my white Triumph Stag because with the other hand I was filming the epic entry with my ciné camera. Once inside the Pavilion there seemed to be an army of old gentlemen directing us round corners, fearful that we might encroach on forbidden territory, such as the gents' loo or the Committee Room.

When I walked into our dressing room I was amazed at the antiquated and delapidated furnishings and fittings: cranky old chipped washbasins, an old washstand-cum-dressing table, bumpy linoleum, and pungent lavatories that smelt of disinfectant. But stepping out on to the players' balcony made me realize what a wonderful cathedral-like calm hung over Lord's in the two hours before a major match. It was a sight I drank in. At last, I was actually going to play at Lord's.

I was shaking with nerves when I walked out to toss with Ann Gordon, the Australian captain. I lost the toss, which in the end turned to our favour. Australia batted first and struggled throughout the opening session as the ball swung and seamed. I was relieved. Had I won the toss, we would have batted first. I was pleased, also, to field first, because it meant that I would be the *first* woman cricketer to step on to the Lord's pitch at the start of the match.

In fact, when I led the team from the dressing room, I was so scared about walking through the Long Room, that I walked right past it and straight through the double doors ahead, turned left behind the seats and then right down the main central steps. No one had actually told me if we *could* go through the Long Room, and for once I was too nervous to challenge tradition. We were greeted on the pitch by a battery of cameras. I felt elated, proud, nervous – and covered with goose pimples. I cried all the way out to the wicket, such was the strength and depth of my emotions. We had arrived!

It was almost cosy out on the pitch and, I thought, much more personal than the wide open spaces at The Oval, Old Trafford and Edgbaston. In the very first over the ground was echoing to our high-pitched appeal as Lorraine Hill, Australia's prolific run-getter (1000 runs and five centuries to her credit on the tour), was caught behind, off the second ball, for a duck. Australia struggled to 161 all out off 59.4 overs. England fielded magnificently. I learnt very rapidly that the ball raced away down the slope to the Tavern and realized how difficult it was to see a lofted shot against the crowd and grandstands.

By the time we batted, a partisan crowd of about 8000 had gathered. We were given a fine run-a-minute start by Enid Bakewell, the Nottinghamshire 'comedian', and Lynne Thomas, Welsh hockey international, who put on 85 for the first wicket, before Enid was run out in a fine old muddle. She had scored an eye-catching 50.

When I went in to bat at number four we were 93 for 2 with 32 overs gone. I scuttled nervously through the Long Room. I could hardly draw spit I was so tense. I took guard, surveyed the field, drew my breath, and the ground was hushed. Suddenly from out of the silence came the piping voice of our son, Ben: 'I can see you, Mummy!' I laughed. I relaxed. I was ready.

I was still batting when the winning boundary was struck by Chris Watmough, our pugnacious Maid of Kent. We put on 69 for the third wicket. One paper described our partnership as first-class entertainment – though I was more sober than usual! Chris struck a drive through mid-wicket for four, completed her fifty, and we passed Australia's score with eight wickets standing and 3.4 overs to spare. The crowd erupted. We ran up the Pavilion steps and the applause and cheers made me cry again. Cries of 'Encore', 'Bravo' and 'Well done, Flinty' rang through the Long Room. It was a memorable moment.

In our dressing room a dozen bottles of champagne waited for us – courtesy of *The Sunday Telegraph* for my 179 against Australia at The Oval a week before. There were no glasses so we drank it from tea-cups.

The only final note of sadness was that MCC made us have the presentation ceremony in the Long Room and not outside the Pavilion on the grass like the men. Only Lord knows why! So all the friends, supporters, families, husbands and children of the players were condemned to watching the presentations through the window. The President of MCC presented the teams with commemorative medallions and a blue cricket ball. In the 1800s women cricketers officially used a blue ball because organizers of country-house cricket felt that cricketing daughters of the landed gentry would swoon at the sight of a red spherical object hurtling towards them! Such Freudian anachronisms are now a thing of the past. Or are they?

Teresa McLean covers cricket for The Financial Times. *She has a cricket Blue from Oxford and Cambridge, and is the author of* Medieval English Gardens *and* The Men in White Coats *(cricket umpires past and present).*

Bread and Butter Pudding

TERESA McLEAN

In some ways Lord's cricket ground is like bread and butter pudding. A dream of a ground – delicious, rich with time-honoured flavours and, on a good day, unbeatable. The first bite, the first sight of the field of play is unforgettable. But too often the whole thing is crusty and heavy. People whose experience of it has been grim can only remember working their way through the outer layers to the dried out, starchy old left-overs at the heart of it all. Worse still is having to say afterwards how lovely it all was, to please the person who introduced them to these secrets, which have been their pride and joy for years.

My feelings about Lord's are as mixed as my feelings about bread and butter pudding, with a strong natural inclination in its favour which is too often disappointed by its performance on the day.

For me, Lord's never quite lives up to its traditions. But I don't know it well. I am a woman, so the MCC ensures that I only know the members' section from the outside looking in, not with the fond familiarity members and grounds develop for each other over the years. I do not go to many matches there and can only write about it from a detached viewpoint, more devoted to its romantic cricketing inheritance than its contemporary matters of fact as they greet a visitor.

The story of the Lord family having their land sequestrated because of their Catholicism and their support for Bonnie Prince Charlie's 1645 rebellion, then Thomas Lord coming south from Yorkshire and ending up as the founder of Lord's cricket ground, used to hold me spellbound with the romantic attraction of the lost cause. Being a Roman Catholic, cricket-loving woman, I have a special sense of solidarity with Thomas Lord's foundation and its survival against the odds.

I have never had that sense of belonging to Lord's in the flesh. It would be unrealistic to expect it. I am a cricket journalist and the vigorous Lord's tradition of contempt for the press came into its own with polite majesty the only time I tried to get into the press box. Festooned with badges and letters of authorization from the newspaper I work for, I was courteously refused entry. I was feeling a bit ordinary and short of glamour at the time and it did wonders for my morale to find myself classed as forbidden fruit without saying or doing anything.

Nor did I mind too much in practical terms because I think the best place to pick up every big ground's atmosphere is on the terraces, enjoying the game alongside the majority of the spectators. I bet most of the Lord's spectators feel in their heart of hearts, as I do, that it should not change fundamentally lest it weaken its personality.

Still, at the same time I could not help feeling a bit sorry for Lord's, that it should feel too nervous to let its noble personality come into its own, genial and splendid, to let cricket-lovers like myself learn more about it. Now that women can play Test matches at Lord's, it has saved itself from withering away into caution that sometimes looks dangerously like bigotry. Maybe, as a gesture of mad panache, it could grant fans with no qualifications except love of the game a privilege such as, say, a guided walk through the members' Pavilion or a guided sitting on a seat outside it, every other leap year or once a decade on Thomas Lord's birthday?*

That would not spoil the atmosphere of moribund repose which is such a precious characteristic of Lord's on quiet days and makes it an oasis of cricketing peace in the desert of urban frenzy all around. It is because I value these traditional characteristics of Lord's so much that I would be sorry to see them retreating into an attitude of defence at all costs, especially as I regard myself as a slightly critical admirer of the ground, not an enemy. I have always liked Lord's and always will like it, but it makes it hard for me to love it.

I love many of its features. The Pavilion is one. It gives the ground its unique feeling of being enclosed, firmly but benignly, against a strong

* Many a true word . . . Lord's tours began officially in May 1990. *Ed.*

backcloth. It is a nice feeling, which gives the crowd a sense of community, watching the game together while the world wastes its time outside.

That feeling is what I remember most vividly about the first time I went to Lord's, to watch Middlesex play in about 1961, though I am not sure of the exact date. My older brother took me and I held his hand tightly as we went through the Grace Gates into the forecourt full of kiosks, pathways, noticeboards, cloakrooms, stairways and all sorts of extra buildings surrounding the field of play itself. I had not been expecting that. I had envisaged myself going through the entrance straight into my seat, overlooking the pitch. The world within a world into which the entrance gates lead is, of course, common to almost all big cricket grounds, but somehow at Lord's it seems to have a particular gift for intensifying the excitement of penetrating through to the game.

The bright green grass helps. I will never forget reaching the brink of the stairs and suddenly seeing the Lord's pitch, green with promises and secrets, for the first time. I am ashamed to admit that I remember little about the game except Fred Titmus bowling and John Murray keeping wicket. Not bad memories though, for a subdued county game playing itself to a dead end nearly thirty years ago.

It was a treat to see spin-bowling used without a second thought, sometimes to attack, sometimes to defend. And as a complement to that, to see a leg-side stumping. Partly, I suppose, these were signs of the times, when medium pace had not yet taken over and dehydrated the game. But they were also a sign of Lord's, where it still seems possible today, as it did then, that a ball might turn a little at any stage of play.

I can well understand the Lord's locals and everyday loyalists who hold it as one of the ground's assets that you never know when the pitch might take spin. It is true. I dare say this reputation contains an element of mystique, but cricket contains an element of mystique, thank God, and if Lord's cannot revel in a bit, we might as well give up and take to football.

I have no local feeling for Lord's to help me pick up indigenous characteristics like bowling sensitivities. If I do feel anything of that sort, it is because I am in love with cricket, not because I am in love with the MCC, Middlesex or Lord's as my home ground. I am not a Londoner. I was born and brought up in Surrey and the romance of walking through St John's Wood on a sunny morning does not sing me neighbourhood songs. I would rather walk through grotty old Kennington on a sunny morning to reach the grotty, friendly old Oval. I am a North London Philistine and Lord's is foreign territory.

That is why I like Lord's best on great occasions, such as Test matches, rather than on gentle, somnolent occasions when the ground is almost empty and the game delights me more than its setting. It is on Test match days that Lord's comes into its own for me, with marvellous panache. I like the new Mound Stand and, as countless cricket romantics have said before me, I know of no sight to match that of a batsman walking down the Pavilion steps on to the pitch at Lord's to inspire the crowd with a classic innings for England. Hope is an important and, I think, a natural virtue in cricket and I shall go on looking forward to the next time I can thrill myself with that sight.

Hilary Mantel, a member of Middlesex, is a brilliant novelist and also the forthright film critic of The Spectator. *'I don't know why I love cricket so much that I'd go anywhere to see it,' she says. 'I never played it myself.'*

If the Glance of a Woman Can Sour Cream . . .

HILARY MANTEL

If you look at cricket writing – I don't mean ghosted memoirs or workaday match reports, but the considered literature of the game – you see at once that its prevailing note is elegiac. The reason for this is not difficult to grasp. Cricket is the most ephemeral of arts. Blink, and you have missed some unique moment. Even a great actor can hope to reproduce his effects, because at least he will arrive again at the same place in his script, with the same line to say. But a batsman plays his stroke only once before it becomes history. A catch is in the air only long enough for you to see it (or not) before the moment of contact (or not) with the palm. There is television, of course, to purvey a second-hand cricket, distorted in time and scale; but your favourite videos wipe themselves out, you find. Only the inner eye can be trusted, and the feeling of belonging to the crowd.

I think it is because of the transience of cricket, its central sad fact, that the cricket-lover grows attached to cricket grounds. On a dark day you can wake up and mutter their names, like a charm, to bring fine weather: Sabina Park, Eden Gardens. The grounds are not inviolate, of course. Sometimes they concrete them over and build hypermarkets. But they cannot, we think, do that to Lord's.

I came to this game lately, or too late anyway to know much about it: unathletic, with no eye for a ball, no head for statistics, and, worst of all, female. Hence my experience of cricket is the experience of a series of exclusions – and mainly the exclusion from proper understanding that playing the game would have brought. Lord's, of course, by barring women from the Pavilion, except under certain special circumstances, perpetrates a most famous exclusion. It is one I cannot bring myself to feel very strongly about, though I wonder about the reasons for it. It is true that applications for MCC membership stretch into the next century, but that is no reason to keep out the female members of Middlesex CCC. One suspects the reasons are not administrative, but atavistic. It cannot be that these days gentlemen fear their view will be blocked by bonnets, or their concentration broken by gusts of piercing chatter about the servant problem or the price of beef. But if, as anciently believed, the glance of a woman can sour cream, it can probably warp willow, crack the pitch, cause umpires' fingers to twitch. Such ancient prejudice must be respected. Lord's must be taken as it is. The Pavilion has its special and masculine atmosphere, its comfortable austerity, its other-worldly air. There is no harm in preserving it for those who can enjoy it. Debarred from a convocation of bishops, one can still pray.

Outside the ambit of privilege, Lord's is an affair of wet plastic seats and the terror of wheel-clampers. Middlesex members have their own room now, made out of part of Q Stand, with great windows that entrap a liquid green light; members will feel, no doubt, a little nostalgia for the time when they had more to complain about. Life outside the Pavilion has its pleasures. You can observe the strange rainwear and even stranger sunwear of the British. You can eavesdrop on conversations, and grow wiser thereby. (Women are supposed not to know how men talk when they're alone. At Lord's they think they're alone.) You can read other people's low newspapers over their shoulders, and be pleasurably shocked by them. You can indulge in the fascinated, horrified inspection of other people's food. And, if I had been in the Pavilion, I would never have seen the small child who, one Sunday a couple of seasons ago, tottered down the steps towards the barrier, held out his arms as if to embrace the fielding side, the umpires and both batsmen, and cried with a beatific smile, 'Daddy!'

True, you can do these things at any cricket ground; though the infant might be a one-off. But Lord's is special: even those who hang about on the fringes of the game, hoping to come back in the next life as a leg-spinner, find themselves consoled by the sense of place, touched by its atmosphere, drawn into the game by its effect on the imagination. As I am a novelist, I could write many semi-meaningful, perhaps not wholly original things about the correspondences between cricket and fiction. Cricket – or any complex, but circumscribed and self-limiting activity – is far more like a novel than life is like a novel. So I can at least persuade myself, when guilt gnaws, that by watching cricket I am actually working, absorbing principles of form and structure and bearing professional witness to the strange machinations of fate.

It is quite usual to think of the game in terms of dramatic spectacle, but in fact a year's cricket, or a Test series, is even more like a novel than it is like a play. The number of characters is large. Their fortunes rise, fall, interweave. People who seemed likely to occupy a line or two decide to stick around and arrogate pages to themselves, perhaps whole strands of the plot. There are climaxes, some of which prove to be illusory. Mere names flower out into human complexity; blind chance plays its part. Just as, in a novel, the fortunes of the protagonist may hang by a thread, or turn on an absurdity, so may the fortunes of a team; and behind the events from hour to hour a certain pattern emerges, which may be discernible only several years on. In a season, you can run through most of the emotions that life produces, and see most of fiction's standard plots work themselves out.

Now, Lord's is the place to entertain these notions. There is a concentrated quality about that arena, a special intensity, a quality of intimacy; this intimacy and intensity touch the non-participants. When you stand in the Pavilion and look at the gate through which the players go out on to the field, a slight intimation of dread flutters behind your ribs, a weak vicarious stage fright. Could that entrance ever, for anyone, become perfectly routine? Possibly. People grow used to anything. But for a moment you can put yourselves into the boots of the player who walks out, you can feel *what it might be like* – and Lord's has performed its trick, it has served its purpose. It has triggered the act of imagination which links together all players, alive and dead, all spectators, every umpire, every groundsman, every bat maker and programme seller, tea-lady and passer-of-the-hat, and puts them at the service of the game.

So then you begin to talk of mystique, of magic, as if the bricks and the grass had something special, though you know cricket is made of people, techniques, time and weather. Again, that pervasive feeling of sadness creeps in, as if beyond the scattered applause you discern the roaring of bulldozers, the fall of a civilization; and it is true that when you discover cricket – if you are one of those people for whom there is a moment of discovery – you are sometimes seized by an irrational fear that it is too good to last, that it will be abolished by some vile government, or that you will be sent away to a country where they don't have it. But there is no real reason, of course, why cricket should induce melancholy. It is best to get out of earshot of what Robertson-Glasgow called 'the strangling fugues of senile jeremiads' and avoid the company of those who ridicule the modern game and are forever reminiscing, about Lord's or any other ground. The best cricket season, in fact, is always the season to come.

For this reason, I like to go past Lord's in winter. I like to be driven past and to catch in the gaps between the grey walls – which might be prison walls – glimpses not of grass but of steel, of meshes and barriers and walkways, the exposed spiny architecture of the stands: so that I can imagine it as a fortress in which is placed, for our own protection, all our virtues, enthusiasms and strengths, and all the best parts of the summer to come.

Michael Meyer would like, I think, to find himself coming in immediately after three ladies. He spends much of his life writing about and translating Ibsen and Strindberg. He says he was once 'an undistinguished and stodgy opening bat who contrived to play regularly for the Old Wellingtonians, Jesters and BBC Bushmen until I was in my late fifties'. He casts some doubt on his stodginess, however, by claiming to be 'the only translator of Ibsen who has hit a six in both Stockholm and The Hague'.

Another Sixty Years On

MICHAEL MEYER

My memories of Lord's stretch back for sixty years, but my association with the ground is twice as long, for my great-great-grandfather, Isaac Montague Marsden, actually owned it from 1860 to 1868. For this he had to thank the incompetence of the MCC Committee. The previous owner, a Mr Dark, had suggested to them that since he was now old they should buy the freehold from him instead of continuing to lease it. They refused, so he sold the ground to Isaac. Six years later the MCC decided they would after all like to own the freehold and, as the Committee minutes show, were scandalized when Isaac demanded a handsome profit on his purchase. Remarks were made about Mr Marsden's original name having been Moses. But they had to pay his price. They could have done with him as Treasurer instead of some of the gentlemen who have filled that office since. Among other accomplishments, he fathered twenty-two children by his two marriages.

I was born within a short walk of Lord's, in Hamilton Terrace, on the first day of the 1921 Test against Australia there, one of the most dismal days of that dismal cricketing summer, though it was less dreadful than 1989, for at least in the Fourth and Fifth Tests in 1921 we achieved honourable draws. (At Manchester we declared at 362 for

4 and bowled out Australia for 175, and at The Oval we again declared at 403 for 8 – Mead 182 not out – though since Tests then lasted for only three days we could not force a win on either occasion.) But at Lord's that Saturday of my birth, 11 June 1921, to quote Neville Cardus, 'England was routed on a perfect wicket for 187, after some three and a half hours of travail, and then the Australians turned our bowlers into batsmen's playthings and at the day's close had scored 191 for 3 wickets.' Woolley's 95 was our only comfort. Cardus tells how in the opening half-hour England lost D. J. Knight, Dipper and Hendren for 25, whereupon Woolley and Johnny Douglas stood firm until lunch, scoring 48 in 154 balls: 25 overs in an hour and a half! The seemingly huge number of runs per day common in Tests then was due, as the bowlers' analyses show, not so much to a higher scoring rate as to the much greater number of overs bowled, averaging around and over twenty an hour.

Isaac's grandson, my great-uncle Ted Marsden, played once or twice for Middlesex in the 1890s as a left-hand quick bowler, one of the few Jews ever to have played first-class cricket (I cannot think of one in my own lifetime apart from Ali Bacher). In 1930, when I was not yet nine, he took me to Lord's to watch England *v* The Rest. That was a great day, for I saw Larwood, Tate, Geary and Robins bowl out The Rest (Jardine, Wyatt, Leyland and Ames among them) for 138; then when England batted, Sutcliffe went early to Maurice Allom, whereupon Hobbs in his forty-eighth year and Hammond, rising twenty-seven, added a glittering hundred before rain stopped play. Not a bad introduction to the game for a schoolboy.

In those far-off 1930s I went more to The Oval than to Lord's because I was a fervent Surrey supporter, for no better reason than that my nurse, who was the most important person in my life, my mother having died when I was small, had been born in the village of Wonersh near Godalming. So Hobbs, Sandham, Fender and Peach were my childhood heroes, rather than Hearne and Hendren. But I attended two pre-war Tests at Lord's, versus Australia in 1938 and West Indies in 1939 – only on the Saturdays, as the matches were played in mid-term. I saw Bradman bowled by Verity for 18 (he played on trying to cut), but missed Verity's famous diving catch in the gully to dismiss McCabe because I was in the Q Stand lavatory. No television Test match highlights then, so the moment was gone forever. Next year George

Headley scored a classical century, but the day was ruined for me by what seemed a blatantly bad lbw decision that saw the end of Constantine when he had scored 14 and had just hit the fast Derbyshire bowler Wilf Copson for two spectacular fours. Thirty years later I found myself playing with Constantine in an Authors *v* National Book League game at Vincent Square, and he confirmed that he felt he was hard done by: 'Copson had a leg slip and the ball was clearly missing leg stump, so I left it.' What pleasure that wretched umpire deprived me and the rest of the crowd of! And sadly when, that August, just before the outbreak of war, Constantine carved the England attack all over The Oval for 79, I was away in Paris.

During the war years I became a frequent visitor to Lord's, for The Oval had been taken over for the duration to serve as a POW camp, and for some reason which I cannot remember or imagine I often watched from the Pavilion. Once Plum Warner seated himself next to me to discuss some article I had written for *The Cricketer*; most of my early efforts in print, apart from those in school or student magazines, appeared there. I came to know Warner quite well. Unlike many of the members then, notably the Secretary, Colonel Rait Kerr, who addressed even senior members as though they were subalterns (he once threatened me with expulsion from the ground for asking Bradman for his autograph after a net), Plum was courteous and genial, even to the young. An extra reason for going to Lord's in wartime was that the food, at any rate in the Pavilion, was better than what was generally available elsewhere in London, a state of affairs that for some reason ceased abruptly on the coming of peace and has never again prevailed.

There were some great contests during and just after the war, one of which caused me unforgettable agony. In 1945 an England XI was playing the Dominions at Lord's. I had to catch a late-afternoon train to Tonbridge and was forced to leave as Constantine strolled in to join, of all batsmen, Keith Miller. Trains were infrequent then and I had no choice, and so I missed one of the most ferocious partnerships ever seen at Lord's, 117 in 45 minutes, including Miller's celebrated six into one of the Pavilion turrets.

There followed the glorious summer of 1947 when Edrich and Compton ran riot, ill preparing us for the disasters of the following year when Bradman's great side destroyed England even more comprehensively than Armstrong's had in 1921. We had one of the strongest opening quartets of batsmen that England can ever have fielded – Hutton, Washbrook, Edrich and Compton – but Lindwall, Miller and Bill Johnson swept them aside. What hopes we had entertained for England that summer, and how those hopes were dashed! Nor had we any bowlers of quality to support Alec Bedser except Douglas Wright with his quick leg-spin, and he had to be used as a stock bowler. Some of those who shared the new ball with Bedser were among the poorest who have ever opened for England, 1989 not excluded (though now that I read the sides we fielded in 1921, some of those openers may have been worse).

Once I became a member in 1950, I began to play tennis regularly at Lord's. I had started the game in 1939 as soon as I left school, on the advice of old Walter Hawes, who had coached me at rackets there. 'You're too slow to be any good at this,' he informed me. 'Take up real tennis. You can be slow at that and get away with it.' Some fearsome characters frequented the Lord's court in the 1950s, not least the professional Jack Groom, who was completely bald and looked exactly like Mr Punch. He had no respect for persons, and shouted at Lord Aberdare and the like just as he did at us. But he had a heart of gold beneath it all and I became very fond of him.

Some of the members were less appealing. One of the fiercest was the novelist A. G. Macdonell, author of *England Their England*. He was very bad at the game and exceedingly ill-tempered on court. If any spectator made the smallest noise in the *dedans* when he was serving, he would turn and bellow, 'How do you expect anyone to play this game without QUIET?' Even worse was Colonel Sam Incledon-Webber, who, as a consequence, I suppose, of his having been a commanding officer, would fix on individual spectators as the objects of his wrath. He would also shout at the marker if the latter allowed even a toe to protrude outside his box: 'Get your feet off the court!' Henry Johns has told me how Incledon-Webber often addressed these words to him, though I doubt if he ever said them to Jack Groom. Fortunately I never played against any of these ogres, apart from one rather crusty old gentleman who was my opponent when the MCC visited Oxford just after the war. But he was not very good, for I beat him without losing a game, so that I did not have to put up with him for long. Tennis players are more civilized now; unless, it occurs to me, young men today feel about me as I did about Macdonell and Incledon-Webber.

More alarming than any of this was an experience I had in the Nursery nets in 1954. A club rabbit, I was being bowled at by some friends when, as in a nightmare, I saw a huge and turbaned man thundering towards the bowler's stump. I recognized him as Mohammed Khan, a member of the Pakistan touring side who was genuinely fast but famously erratic. At first I thought he must surely be going to bowl to someone in the adjoining net. But no, I was his target, and he flung down a short-pitched ball which narrowly missed my jaw. I could not imagine why he should be bowling at me, and did not dare to ask. It was no use backing away to square leg, for the ball was just as likely to go there as straight. But after two or three similar deliveries, all of which whistled around my chest or head, Mohammed rubbed his thigh, cried, 'Is still not good', and departed. I then recalled having read that he had been out with a pulled muscle. Never have I been so glad to hear that someone's injury had not healed. I doubt if any batsman in the long history of Lord's has been as frightened as I was that afternoon.

Inevitably there have been many changes at Lord's since I first went there sixty years ago: the Warner Stand, the new Mound Stand, the advertisement boards everywhere (what a to-do there was when these were first mooted!), the electronic scoreboard, even the public-address system, the sight-screen in the Pavilion (there was none at that end pre-war), the autograph hunters behind the Pavilion (Colonel Rait Kerr must be turning in his grave), the absence of hats and caps in the crowd (hardly anyone went bareheaded then), the disappearance of the Tavern, the tall blocks heightening the skyline outside. The best change has been that all the cricketers emerge from the Pavilion instead of, as then, the amateurs down the steps and the professionals from where the Pavilion now joins the Warner Stand. What I miss most is the big attendances we had each Saturday even for quite minor matches (9000 watched Oxford *v* Cambridge on that day in 1939, ten times as many as attend today).

By the time these lines appear, the Nursery End will have been remodelled, too. Only the Pavilion, the Grandstand, Q Stand, the playing area and the tennis court will be as they were sixty years ago. Yet somehow all these changes seem only cosmetic. Lord's remains Lord's.

Like Michael Meyer, David Benedictus is a literary figure whose cricketing reach exceeds his grasp. He has always seemed to specialize in succès de scandale *ever since his first novel* The Fourth of June, *and most recently achieved it by being the BBC man responsible for having* Lady Chatterley's Lover *read on 'Book at Bedtime'.*

Milton, Marlow, Milburn and Me

DAVID BENEDICTUS

I was small for my age and weedy. I had an incipient paunch, the result, I believe, of the strange system at Stone House, Broadstairs, for eliminating – or failing to eliminate – bodily waste. After breakfast, which usually contained porridge because the headmaster had Scottish origins and was very much in the John Buchan mould, we retired to our classroom and then, as our numbers were read out, to the 'rears' where, ignoring the schoolboy graffiti and trying to ignore the spy-holes, we would strain to keep ourselves regular. Always something of an iconoclast, I was either unwilling or unable – and probably both – to perform to order.

My pasty appearance and improbable shape did not make for instant popularity, and when, during the early days of my first summer term – the summer of 1947, the hottest of summers following the coldest of winters and the most flood-ridden of springs – an opportunity for public heroics presented itself, I was not going to let it pass. Allerton, the fast bowler for the First XI, had issued a challenge. Was there amongst us one so bold as would be prepared to stand up to his bowling against the side of the nets on Upper Field? Without pads or gloves? Indeed there was. This 'pot-bellied geranium' (where on earth did the noun come from? Charles Peters, I expect. He always had an original mind, and was quick and apt with nicknames) piped up bravely, and murmurs of approval rose above the snoek and cocoa.

How fast was Allerton? He seemed the fastest thing on two legs, but it may have been that the long run-up, with its successful intention of prolonging the moment, and the coincidence that he shared a name with the terrifying matron added several imagined miles an hour to his delivery. I remember being struck on the shins by a speedy leg-cutter. But I would have remembered it whether or not it had happened. I survived.

The biggest day of the cricketing year was the fathers' match. For this the fathers had to use special bats, narrowed right down to the splice, and one's status at school was largely dependent on paternal prowess. In 1947, with severe petrol rationing still in force, many fathers were unable to make the occasion and the side was bolstered with one or two masters. I cannot remember whether my father played, though we were to play on the same side in the school holidays for Cookham Dean. It was not easy for the fathers. They were required by their sons to do well, and required by the school to lose by a narrow margin.

As a cricketer myself I had two talents. At silly point I was a demon and snapped up everything that came my way. It was not, of course, silly point in those days, just point, and I stood so close that I could all but pluck the ball off the dead bat of the opposing batsman. And I was a resolute opening bat. I had two shots: I could run the ball down through the slips or I could turn it off my legs. So renowned was I for scoring behind the wicket that when once, in a moment of passion, I struck the ball through extra cover to the boundary, Mr Winser led the cheers. It was the first time I had been known to score in front of the wicket.

Mr Winser, the English master, took cricket. He had long floppy hair forever tumbling into his eyes, and he affected a Bohemian manner in other ways. One term he acquired some glamour in our eyes by appearing in a production of *Comus* at a local venue. Milton in Margate perhaps? It seems improbable. Mr Winser was a partial umpire, and I believe on reflection that he had a soft spot for me, a promising English scholar. I clearly recall being struck on the pads while plumb in front of the wicket. There was a long, Miltonic pause. If it had been old chain-smoking Mr Buckworth, who taught us Latin and Greek, at the bowler's end, his nicotine-stained finger would have been up at once. I looked at Wiz and Wiz looked at me. Ever so delicately I adjusted my position, leaning further and further to the off, until my pads must have been clearly outside the line of the stumps, by which time Mr Winser could in all conscience shake his head and intone, 'Not out'.

During the holidays there were cricket matches between the Marlow Mothers and the Henley Mothers. The mothers did not play, of course, but the games were the inspiration of the mothers and tended to be imposed on their reluctant sons. Never were matches so keenly fought! Not, again, by the boys. They were not cricketers, and these matches were the bane of the holidays. But the mothers, cajoling from the sidelines, engaged passionately in debates about the state of the ground, the state of the weather (it usually rained), and the appalling standards of umpiring. For no Henley boy was ever fairly out, and no Marlow boy could possibly have been caught off the glove. The boys were all mediocre cricketers with the exception of John McDermott, our fast bowler and future IBM executive, and the Henley mothers certainly did not take kindly to John bowling too long or too hard. The boys would be caught out, bowled out, run out, and would return reluctantly to the pavilion; reluctant because they would have liked to bat on, doubly reluctant because their mothers would be waiting for them, to drive them back on to the field of play to the accompaniment of: 'Was that out? It didn't look out to me!'

In the holidays came the visits to the Lord's Tests. The new scorebook, the sharpened pencil, the determined recording of every ball bowled, every run scored. The good times when the Bedser twins were together – Alec who took wickets and Eric who helped. They were fast and dependable and it was a very special foreign tourist who dared to take a long handle to them. The added thrill when Compton joined Edrich; the speed and ferocity of Wes Hall; the insouciance of Colin Milburn, whose opening thrashes never lasted long, but while they did. . . . (He and Pataudi both lost eyes in accidents. Why could they not have shared one between them and continued to bat like the angels they were?) Hutton was a bore and so was Trevor Bailey, but not Ken Barrington. Slow though he was at times, there was something about that ugly mug, those broad shoulders, that square-on stance that gave confidence to all. He was not a gent, but you could depend on Ken, and while others came and went, if he remained, there was always hope. Once the selectors dropped him for scoring too slowly. What would they not give for a Ken Barrington today? Trueman was tremendous, but there was something even more heroic about Statham. Was it my imagination or did he always have to bowl into the wind? Line and length, line and length, all morning long, no matter how desperate the situation. Then the spinners, Wardle and Lock and Laker, with Godfrey Evans behind the wicket, hurling himself dementedly to leg to catch a ball maybe 15 yards to his left. If it wasn't fifteen it seemed like it. And that innings on the morning of the Lord's Test with all the recognized batsmen gone when Evans thrashed them all over the field: 98 before lunch, I think it was, and I was there! Any self-respecting umpire would have allowed another over, but in my heart I feel that Evans would not have welcomed it. Fairly or not at all, that's how he would have wanted his pre-prandial century.

For years as an adult I used images of Lord's to get off to sleep (I still do). I am walking down the steps of the Pavilion in front of a full house to open the batting for England. I am never clear as to the identity of my number two, but it scarcely matters. I play such flashing stuff, 15 or 16 off the first 2 overs, and then . . . well, by then I am asleep.

I became a wicket-keeper. In the early 1960s I played for the 'Z Cars' team against the Director General's XI. The DG was not too sprightly at mid-off, so that when he batted our bowlers bowled gently at him. Good career move. He carted the ball about a bit so finally we brought on Alan Moss, the Middlesex fast bowler and our tame professional; a few lobs and long-hops followed and then the guvnor hit over a straight one. 'Well,' I heard him say as he strode from the wicket, 'at least it took a professional to get me out!'

As a journalist I interviewed Asif Iqbal, Alan Knott and Mike Brearley. Brearley told me that while he was waiting for a fast bowler to bowl he would hum to himself the first few bars of the Razumovsky Overture; Knotty spoke of his struggles to keep fit; Asif of the English weather. I liked being around cricketers. I spent a day in the BBC commentators' box once. Christopher Martin-Jenkins took me out to tea. 'When you write about us, you will say how much *nicer* we are than footballers, won't you?' They are. I said I would, and I did. Once I was invited to spend the Saturday of a Lord's Test in a private box. The invitation came from a very rich man nearer seven feet tall than six. He wanted, I think, to know what were my intentions towards his beautiful daughter. Her skyscraper brothers were there, too. My intentions were not entirely honourable and I never saw the girl again.

It had not occurred to me that one day I might actually play at Lord's, and I never did; but I did play in the Lord's nets. It came about in this way. I was working at Channel 4 and each season we played just one match against Thames Television. Because we were so rusty it was incumbent upon us to have a warm-up, and someone at the Channel had influence, I suppose. So into the Lord's nets we went. It felt extraordinary, and I drove the ball off my toes with uncharacteristic fluency.

We beat Thames that year. Jeremy Isaacs arrived at tea-time, when I was not out, and I explained to him that, if I continued batting, it was unlikely that I would make the plane that was to take me from Heathrow to Rome for a European drama co-production meeting. Which was more important, I enquired – European co-production or beating Thames? 'Beating Thames, of course,' replied the boss, and I felt proud to be working for an organization which had its priorities so clearly delineated. I continued batting and hit the winning run, later hitch-hiking a ride on an Air India flight that touched down in Rome for refuelling. The co-production meeting led to 'The Manageress', a soccer series, I'm afraid.

There was a picture of Denis Compton in a colour magazine recently. He looked plump and dozy and his twelve-year-old daughter was complaining that he makes her play cricket in the garden and insists on hogging the batting. He always did, as I recall. It brought back those Lord's afternoons, so I turned again to an old schoolboy scorebook and there he was and all the other heroes' names. As I flipped through the pages I could taste again the marge in the ham sandwiches and the doubtful flavour of the orange squash from the same old thermos, and see again the ball as it hopped over the turf towards me, while Colin Milburn grinned at his partner, or Ted Dexter raised his bat ever so elegantly in the air.

Opposite Lord's in the St John's Wood Road is the synagogue where once a year I atone for my sins. It is being rebuilt. There was some discussion about what sort of a building should replace the fine old and dignified one, and what sort of facilities it should provide. In my heart of hearts I thought: why not give it a tunnel to Lord's and, if ever Hick is in full flight, stop atoning for a while and go and watch the glory that ensues when God and man work together in full co-operation. In the sunlight. In the summer. Like the old days.

Michael Davie, formerly of the Observer, *shares journalism with David Benedictus and also edited the excellent* Faber Book of Cricket *with his son, Simon. Unlike Benedictus he is not a novelist, but his contribution here veers disturbingly towards fiction. It's so far-fetched, however, that it has to be true.*

Groucho in the Club

MICHAEL DAVIE

Drinking Guinness in a Fleet Street pub one evening in the summer of 1954, John Gale and I – both of us reporters on the *Observer* – saw in the *Evening Standard* that Groucho Marx had arrived at the Savoy Hotel; he was quoted as saying that he was already bored.

John Gale, now dead, like Groucho, was sometimes impetuous. Also, despite his conventional appearance, he was strongly drawn to the bizarre; he knew the Marx Brothers films almost by heart, though not as well as I did. Now he threw down the *Standard* and, with a wild glint in his eye, exclaimed: 'If he's bored, why don't we entertain him? We'll take him to Lord's!' We were both MCC members; John was a good bat and had a terrific throw. 'It would make a good piece,' I said. 'No, no!' said John. 'We must promise not to write about it. That's the whole point!'

He pulled a notebook out of his pocket and scribbled: 'Dear Mr Marx – We see from the papers that you are bored. If so, we would like to take you to see a cricket match tomorrow afternoon. We would not write about it.' We added the office address, telephone number and signatures, tore the page out of the notebook and took it round to the desk at the Savoy, where we had another, slightly hysterical drink and went home.

Next morning John was sitting at his desk when the phone rang. 'Mr Gale? This is Mr Marx.' John had no idea who it was. 'Er . . . Mr Marx?' 'You sent me a note asking me to a cricket game.' John stood

up. Arrangements were made. We were to pick him up at the Berkeley Hotel, where he was lunching, at 2.30 p.m. John hung up. We looked anxiously out of the window; at least it wasn't raining. We looked at the nearest sports page: MCC *v* Cambridge University; second day. The dimmest game of the season! Still, it meant there would be plenty of room.

On the way to the Berkeley by taxi, we threw our notebooks out of the window. When we got there we sent in our names via the head waiter and sat down on gilt chairs in an anteroom. There was no denying our joint nervousness, even though we had both previously encountered, as reporters, people just as famous as Groucho. For instance, we once came across – again at Lord's, funnily enough – Boris Karloff. Gale had danced with the Queen.

But we were edgy, and, as it turned out, rightly so. The great man came out of the buttery at speed. He was wearing a Gene Sarazen golf cap, light raincoat, and brown brogues. He had a moustache, but not his black screen moustache: his real one was short and bristly. He walked with a definite lope, which seemed natural, not put on, though again much less pronounced than his screen lope. In his wake but plainly accompanying him came a strikingly pretty girl: we had not expected that. Our plan had been to take him into the Pavilion. 'This is my secretary, Miss Hartford,' he said. 'One of the Connecticut Hartfords. Did you bring the Benzedrine?'

We had kept the taxi waiting. Gale and I sat on the jump seats. Mr Marx and Miss Hartford sat on the other seat, saying nothing. I felt the need to talk and explain. 'I'm afraid it isn't a very important game,' I said. 'It's Cambridge University against the Marylebone Cricket Club. This is the second day of a three-day match and it's like baseball, with one team batting and one fielding. MCC – that's Marylebone – will be batting and Cambridge will be fielding.'

'Fielding?' said Mr Marx, continuing to look out of the window, but suddenly alert. 'Didn't he write *Tom Brown's Schooldays*?'

I was confused. 'Um, well, I suppose. . . .' I began to wonder about Gale's bright idea. Mr Marx was showing no gratitude for our altruistic initiative, and seemed jumpy and aggressive.

At the Grace Gates, he got out on the street side and Miss Hartford on the pavement side. Gale spoke to Miss Hartford and I paid, and as we did so we became aware that Mr Marx had walked round the back of the cab and was getting in again on the pavement side. The cab driver thought he was a new fare, pulled down his flag and prepared to drive off. Mr Marx then got out, not smiling, as if he had put the cab driver in his place, too.

Gale and I made slightly hearty remarks, to which Miss Hartford, though not Mr Marx, responded. He looked at the notice at the back of Q Stand. '"Members and Friends". That's the most ambiguous notice I've ever seen.' Nothing he had said so far seemed to lend itself to a reply.

We went into P Stand. The day was fine but overcast, the ground virtually empty: one young man a dozen rows behind us; a group in front of the Tavern. A Cambridge slow bowler was wearing a bright blue turban. Mr Marx now showed some interest in learning about the game and its rules, saying he liked and watched baseball. The differences were explored. Mr Marx was especially interested to hear that the Tavern served drink all afternoon, while ordinary pubs were closed; he wondered in that case why the crowd wasn't bigger: a good question. Then Gale asked him if he'd like to inspect the Pavilion.

He gave me an account later. To be discreet, he signed Groucho in as 'Mr G. Marx', but the doorman had recognized him and mentioned that they had had other well-known American gentlemen in the Pavilion before – was Cary Grant one of them? Then his excitement had evidently got the better of him, because soon after Gale and Mr Marx went into the Long Room a high MCC official appeared, alerted by the doorman, and introduced himself. Mr Marx still had on his golfing cap and by this time was smoking a 6-inch cigar. Then the official made a social error. 'Are you on holiday here, Mr Marx?' he enquired. The hint of condescension in his voice was surely unintentional, but Gale thought he detected it, and Mr Marx certainly did. He looked at the official, took the cigar out of his mouth, and continued to look at him, right between the eyes. 'I was until I saw this game,' he said. The official soon withdrew, and Gale apologized. 'Don't worry,' said Mr Marx. 'I've met stuffed shoits before.'

Gale showed him the painting of a long-haired young man leaning on a bat. 'Cricket, eh? 1789, eh? I guess this homo thing started earlier than we thought.'

Back in P Stand, where Miss Hartford had proved an easy companion, it seemed time to leave. As we stood up, the young man who had been sitting alone a dozen rows behind came bashfully forward proffering a pencil and scorecard. 'It is Mr Groucho Marx, isn't it?' he asked. Mr Marx took the pencil and began to sign. Then he stopped, and looked at the young man. 'Were you the guy making all the noise back there?' His timing was exact. The young man, who had been leaning forward to see the signature, took an alarmed step back. 'Why, no!' he said, then gave a weak smile. No smile from Mr Marx, however.

Coming away we met the novelist Philip Toynbee, and all piled into the same taxi. Mr Marx soon established that Philip was the son of Professor Arnold Toynbee, then at the height of his international fame, especially in the United States, as the historian of the cyclical nature of civilizations. He asked Philip what it was like to be the son of such a famous father. Philip told a story of his delight, visiting Turkey, when a Turk asked him if he was the famous Toynbee, and Philip had said wearily, no, that was Arnold, his father, and the Turk had cried, 'No, no! I mean Philip Toynbee! The author of *Tea With Mrs Goodman*!' Mr Marx said it must be very difficult. His own son Arthur had found it necessary to leave the United States altogether and settle in Paris, where he worked as a tennis coach. I could sympathize with Arthur's problem, and silently remembered S. J. Perelman saying he would 'rather be whipped naked down the Rue de Rivoli' than work as a scriptwriter on another Marx Brothers film.

My Editor later wrote to Groucho, asking him if he'd like to review books for the paper. Groucho declined, saying he had so many irons in the fire at the moment that there was practically no fire. He added: 'If you encounter either or both of those charming gents who escorted me to the cricket fields of England last summer, give them my best. I must say it was one of the most restful afternoons I've ever experienced.'

The Dead Ringer

MAX DAVIDSON

Was he or wasn't he? I could never be certain and I don't think I wanted to be certain because the mystery added a piquancy which the cricket lacked. It was the perfect seasoning to an afternoon at Lord's.

He sat in the middle tier of the Pavilion, a still, slightly tense figure hunched forward in his seat to watch the play. He must have been over seventy when I first saw him and had the look of a country member, with his tweed suit and his sandwiches and his battered binocular-case slung over his shoulder. He never applauded or showed any sign of emotion but, as soon as a wicket fell, he would take out a biro and enter the details meticulously on his scorecard. He was always on his own; and, if he wasn't Laurence Olivier, he was the deadest ringer for Laurence Olivier I had ever seen in my life.

The hair was the same. The eyes were the same. The mouth and lips, with their delicacy and their lurking roguishness, were identical. And if the hooked nose was more suggestive of Richard III than Henry V, was it out of the question that the grand old master of disguise should dip into his make-up box to escape detection?

That Olivier was a member of the MCC I knew from theatrical reference books. So was Ralph Richardson. So was Harold Pinter. Indeed, I'm not sure that one of my motives for joining the club wasn't

the prospect of hobnobbing with such luminaries in the hallowed surroundings of the Long Room. I must have been extraordinarily naïve, for the Pavilion at Lord's plays host to some of the worst bores in London; and it wasn't long before I was dodging 'old friends' as fast as the English batsmen were ducking West Indian bouncers in the middle.

Now, at last, to offset the surrounding ennui, was the great man himself. Or was it? For literally years I could never make up my mind. Some days the resemblance was slight; others it was overwhelming. And if it was unlikely that our finest actor should spend so many Saturdays watching cricket, it wasn't impossible; stranger things had happened.

Armed with this mad, despairing hope, I would seek out my man when I got to the ground and, from a discreet vantage point, study him. I examined his right profile. I examined his left profile. I looked at him from behind. Once I followed him right round the ground during the lunch interval, hoping for a clue in the way he walked: Olivier had a distinctive walk. No luck. It could have been and, there again, it couldn't. Nobody else looked at him twice, but this didn't bother me: it would only make my perspicacity more remarkable if I was proved correct.

I even dragged friends along for a second opinion. Most of them took one look and laughed or told me I was mad. But then an old Austrian crony – he was blind in one eye, ignorant of the British theatre, but couldn't bear to disappoint anyone – stood there thoughtfully with his hands on his hips and said, 'Jesus, Max, you just *could* be right.' It was all the corroboration I needed.

In 1981 the mystery very nearly reached a dénouement. I was standing in the gangway as usual, with one eye on my man and one on the game, when the seat next to him became vacant; I hesitated, then slipped into it. Close to, my impression was of a rather farmyardy smell, but this was neither here nor there: the reference books were silent about what Olivier smelled like. It was no good: I would have to take the bull by the horns and get him to *talk*.

Tricky, very tricky. I was far too timid to say, 'Excuse me, aren't you. . . ?' and, if I tried any funny business, like muttering Shakespearian quotations under my breath, the stewards would chuck me out. So it had to be subtler. Perhaps the starting point should be cricket, since he obviously enjoyed the game? Unfortunately, Geoffrey Boycott was batting and conversational openings sparse. Maiden followed maiden, punctuated by the odd pushed single. A soporific calm descended and my friend's eyes nodded shut. . . .

Suddenly, miracle! A long-hop from Alderman, a flashing square cut and Boycott had registered his first boundary after an hour and a half. Loud applause, mostly ironic. I cleared my throat and turned my head. 'He can really put away the bad ball, can't he?' Not very scintillating, but I've heard worse from Richie Benaud on a bad morning and he gets paid for it. The man opened his eyes and looked at me. 'Hrrrrmph!' he gargled, sounding like a retired brigadier after a kipper had gone down the wrong way. It wasn't much to go on: I had hoped for an iambic pentameter. Then Boycott hit another boundary and pandemonium broke loose. 'You've got to admire the man, haven't you?' I shouted, throwing caution to the winds.

And then it happened. His nostrils quivered, his eyes flashed, and he gave me a Look. One of those proud, withering, take-any-liberties-and-I'll-have-you-for-breakfast looks which had made him such an incomparable actor. 'A sense of danger' was how Kenneth Tynan described the quality which put him head and shoulders above his contemporaries. My God, how right he was! I shut my mouth, waited till the end of the over and tiptoed to a different seat. In later years my doubts returned and I veered back to the view that the man was just a plausible look-alike. But at that moment, on that afternoon, I had no doubts. *I knew.*

Olivier died in July 1989 and one detail leapt out at me from the obituary notices. Right up to the end of his life, apparently, he liked to potter down to his Sussex local, sit in the corner with a pint of beer in his hand and just *fade into the background.* Unaccompanied, unnoticed, and no doubt pleased as Punch with his momentary anonymity. The story seemed to confirm all my theories.

Two weeks later I was at Lord's and, in some trepidation, climbed the stairs to the Pavilion balcony. Deep down, I must have realized that a mystery which had given me pleasure for years was about to be solved, and not in the way I wanted; but I wasn't prepared for the wave of disappointment which swept over me when I saw my man in his usual place. Robbed of his borrowed greatness, he looked impossibly, painfully nondescript: he could no more have played Hamlet or King

Lear than hit a six over the Pavilion. I felt like a callow youth who had given his heart to a woman and woken, in his maturity, to her terrible ordinariness. At least Boycott wasn't still batting.

*Simon Raven is a novelist and his is a work of fiction. A short story
seemed a good idea halfway through the writing order. Raven was
a very useful cricketer who played in the same Charterhouse XI as
Peter May and is still a member of MCC, Butterflies and Trogs.*

The Team Photograph

SIMON RAVEN

The photograph of the school First XI taken at the end of July 1945
was not of eleven boys but of twelve. This was because Otho de
Freville, the head of the school, had bullied Frank Rawlings, captain of
cricket, into awarding a twelfth cap, which went to Otho himself. This
honour Otho had done nothing to deserve except to play as a substitute
against Eton, which is to say that he fielded (in a fashion) for about 32
minutes before the match was murdered just after noon, by rain.

That was in June. Weeks later, a day or two before 'Colour Sunday'
(when the caps for all the XIs were finally made up and announced),
Otho said to Frank Rawlings, 'A fellow who was chosen to take the
field against Eton deserves his First XI cap.'

'It was your only match,' said Frank Rawlings, 'and you weren't
chosen. You were a substitute for Daniel Spinoza, who unfortunately
had to be away.'

And even that, as Frank remarked to me later when reporting the
conversation, was a euphemistic statement of the affair. In fact, Otho
had gone round and about, some days before the Eton match, telling
everyone that Spinoza looked too 'foreign' to be allowed to represent
the school against Eton. It would be all right in most other matches,
Otho conceded – against Westminster or Harrow, if not, perhaps,
against Winchester; but most definitely not in the match against Eton.
Yes, yes, Otho quite understood that Spinoza was our only left-arm
spin-bowler and was also a useful batsman at number seven or eight

(provided the opposition's fast men had been taken off); but when it came to the fixture against Eton such considerations must give way to those of social propriety. It simply was not proper to allow someone as . . . er . . . *swarthy* as Spinoza to turn out on this occasion.

For a time Frank Rawlings deprecated this disgraceful sentiment; but Daniel Spinoza himself, a retiring and scholarly boy, had been so disturbed by all the talk that he eventually told Frank that he would, in any case, be away during the Eton match for an interview with an Appointments Board, though everyone knew very well (because others were to attend it) that the Board did not commence until the afternoon of the day after the match and that Spinoza could easily have made the journey to London that morning. All of us, however, whether in the XI or not, maintained a discreet (or shifty) silence in the matter; and so Otho played instead, or at least sauntered about on the field in his beautifully pressed and laundered kit, until the rains came.

In subsequent matches, Spinoza resumed his place; he finished the season with a bowling average of 9.3 (20 wickets at a cost of 186) and a batting average of 16.6 recurring (highest score 41 not out), and had indeed received his cap in mid-June, not long after the infamous Eton affair. Spinoza's cap was the nineth of the XI; the tenth and eleventh were awarded in early July; and all eleven capped players were warned to appear at three of the afternoon on 'Colour (or Capping) Sunday' for the First XI photograph.

'Give twelve caps and give me the twelfth,' Otho had said to Frank Rawlings on the Thursday before. 'I want to be in that photo on Sunday. It will make a fitting end to my career in this place.'

'I can only award eleven caps,' Frank Rawlings said, 'and I have already done so.'

'You are captain of cricket and you can do what you wish. Even the Head Man cannot interfere. If anyone makes a row, you can always say that I did, when all is said, play against Eton.'

Et cetera. Et cetera. Frank Rawlings was a tired man (after the whole season, after gruelling exams) and he wanted peace. Otho was a persistent man who could and would, at a need, make trouble. It was time for all to part, thought Frank, without discordance; the whole thing would in any case be forgotten by the following September, when men's minds turned to football and he himself would be far away (albeit the war in Europe was now over) serving his king.

So Frank agreed. Otho was posted on the early morning of 'Colour Sunday' (the last of the school year) as being the twelfth of the First XI caps. That afternoon, when the photograph was taken in front of the pavilion, five men sat for it in the front row as usual, and seven stood behind them instead of six.

Spinoza arrived late and hustled into the standing line of seven just inside Otho, although he should, such was his seniority, have been standing in the middle of the row and not next to Otho, who as last cap of all was at the end of it.

'Just a minute,' said Otho to the photographer, 'this boy on my left should be much further in. I don't want him anywhere near me.'

'Does it matter?' said the photographer. 'I believe there is a world war on, or was until the other day. Although it is a Sunday, I have more important things to do than humour the fads of pampered boys.'

(The 'post-war spirit', you see, was catching on fast.)

Now, Spinoza could well have moved into his right place while the photographer was asserting himself with this speech, but apparently he chose not to; and so the photograph was taken with Otho outside Spinoza on the left (as you looked at it) of the back row. Then the First XI of 1945 shook hands, with just a tear or two, and went on their ways . . . all except for Daniel Spinoza, who did indeed go on his way, but shed no tear and shook no hand.

And now it is 1985, forty years on (as the song has it), and Otho de Freville is dead. Since he has made quite a mark as a publisher of technical books, his obituary in *The Daily Telegraph* (on a thin day for deaths) is prominent. There is also a picture, in which Otho looks a bit flea-bitten. So I have hunted out my copy of the First XI photograph of 1945 in order to remind myself, out of interest rather than affection, what Otho had looked like on the verge of his spunky youth.

He isn't there. Spinoza is there, but now he is at the end of a back row of six boys only.

How very peculiar. I am sure I have remembered correctly all the things I have just been telling you. Otho *must* be there; only he isn't. I do hope my memory hasn't collapsed. I could have sworn, even after forty years. . . . No good worrying. Next week I shall be seeing Frank Rawlings at Lord's. We always meet at the Lord's Test. I shall ask him if he remembers what I remember, and if so, whether he can explain the thing.

'Well, now,' said Frank Rawlings this afternoon at Lord's. 'For a start, *I* haven't got a copy of that photo. My wife Lileth threw it away. She is jealous of my past, which of course includes you: so I told her the firm was sending me to Birmingham for the day. I only hope she doesn't see me sitting here on television. Where was I?'

'Our old team photograph.'

'Oh, yes. Several times over the years, however, I have seen a copy of it in magazines or newspapers. After all, it includes an England cricketer, a judge of appeal, and about the only politician of probity the country has had for thirty years. So one sees it from time to time in the public prints. Always, as far as I recall, it has shown Otho de Freville and Daniel Spinoza standing together, at the end of the back row, Spinoza being inside Otho.'

'Just as I remember from the day it was taken,' I said.

'But now you say that your copy no longer includes Otho?'

'Gone. Clean gone.'

A grey, stooping, seedily dressed man worked his way along our row and inserted himself on the bench in the yard or so we had left between us for comfort.

'Steady on, sir,' I said. 'There's not room for the three of us.'

'Enough,' he said, 'for an old companion. Daniel Spinoza.'

'Spinoza?' said Frank. 'I haven't seen you since—'

'Since 1945,' said the newcomer. 'Nor has Raven here. I have been in another country. In the East . . . whence my family came. I hated this country . . . where people said things about me such as de Freville once said. And no one, not one of you in the XI, stood up for me. I hated you all, more and more over the years, when I took out that photograph to look at you . . . in another country, in the East. Yes, I hated you all; but I hated de Freville the most.'

'And yet,' I said, 'you stood next to him in the photograph. You needn't have done, you shouldn't have done, but you did.'

'I had my reasons. Proximity among them.' He was, I reflected, tiresomely proximate to Frank and myself now. 'Of course, we were young then,' he went on, 'and there was no hurry. After forty years time is running short. Things are changing fast, now that I am back again from that other country in the East. Go home, Raven: go home and look at that photograph.'

'I have,' I said.

'Go home and look again. Why didn't you stand up for me, for your companion? None of you did,' he muttered, and began to rise.

'I stood up for you,' said Frank.

'Yes. A little. Not for long. You breathed the same sigh of relief as the rest of them when I made my excuse. I remembered that, all those hours in the East I spent looking at that photograph of my companions. But you were the best of them. Not like de Freville with his malice, or Raven here, with his indifference.'

He began to shamble away along the row. Then he looked back.

'Go home and look again,' he called in a high voice, 'at the XI of 1945.'

So now I am looking again.

Spinoza is grinning. Next to him, where Otho de Freville once was and then was not, a kind of waxwork is standing, of a figure wearing beautifully pressed white flannel trousers and a fine silk shirt, both of a quality so difficult to obtain during the war, and both now stained by some sort of oozing flux.

I myself am sitting where I sat on that July afternoon, at the end of the first row, just in front of the grinning Spinoza. I, too, am grinning, but not in the same manner as Spinoza. As I look at myself in the photograph, I am fascinated by the tufts and blotches on my slimy pate where, surely, forty years ago, there had been bright auburn waves . . . where, even now, there is a healthy brown growth. Or is there? Very soon I must go and look into the glass.

A small group of cricketers have appeared at Lord's as very young men indeed. Not many of them are what you might call men of letters, but these next two most certainly are. The first, John Letts, used to run the Folio Society, famous for its beautifully produced versions of fine books. He is now the boss of the Trollope Society, dedicated to that most English of English writers.

A Question of Upbringing

JOHN LETTS

Last year I paid my first visit to Lord's for forty years. I made this pilgrimage, late in October, partly to visit the Cricket Memorial Gallery and partly to look again at the scene of some rather curious highlights from my early life.

Much was changed. I think only Thomas Verity's splendid 1890 Pavilion – rose red, like the city of Petra – and Sir Herbert Barker's 1925 Grandstand have survived. Before making my way to the Memorial Gallery behind the Pavilion, I eluded the officials for a second and slipped along the narrow passageway between the Pavilion and the new Q Stand.

It was a curiously disappointing sight. The old stands which flanked the Pavilion had gone. The Nursery End was totally occupied by bulldozers, concrete mixers and builders' mess. The low elegant Victorian stand curving away to the right of the Pavilion was a loss I particularly regretted. No doubt the new stands will make the place more modern, more economic to run; but it will be more like a baseball stadium. Very admirable: but not exactly the place I hoped to see. I breathed a sigh of resignation.

The Gallery itself, in the autumn, seemed a little austere, even clinical. There is a portrait of Sydney Barnes, which makes him look

suitably ferocious. There are rows and rows of dead bats: some curved, some autographed, some with commemorative silver shields on them. One is the famous bat which belonged to Albert Trott, 'Albatrott', an export from Australia, who was said to have developed a prodigious break by practising endlessly against a packing case labelled G. Giffen. He it was who hit a ball right over Verity's Pavilion, only nine years after it was built: a feat which has never to this day been emulated. There are many balls, suitably inscribed. The one that jogged my memory was that surmounted by a modest stuffed sparrow. It was despatched – I did not need to read the caption – by a ball bowled by Jahangir Khan to Tommy Pearce on 3 July 1936. If it was engraved in my mind, that was because I remember reading it in the new *Wisden* for 1937, when I was eight, an age when I read the new issue within days of publication.

One of the pictures caught my eye. It was a large oil painting of the scene at Lord's in a Test match in 1938, made over the five days by that excellent and under-rated painter Charlie Cundall. His Lord's certainly *was* my Lord's. There was the ramshackle growth of buildings, red-bricked and turreted, where the new Q Stand sits impersonally today. There was the real Tavern, which bears little resemblance to today's impostor. And I could add what the caption fails to tell us: that this was the Test match, so beautifully recorded, in which Wally Hammond made a majestic 240 – 80 runs, memory tells me, in each session.

I fell to wondering where all this information came from. It took me back to a kind of childhood which today would be so rare as to be abnormal, if it is not actually extinct. The late Bertie Farjeon once revealed that, when he was a small boy, he used to pray each night for Surrey. In my case, the subject of my hopes for divine intervention was Gloucestershire: though I am not sure how often I *prayed*. Farjeon said, 'There was a time (pardon my boasting) when I knew not only the initials but the Christian names of all the professionals: and when, at the corner of the Adelaide and Winchester Roads in South Hampstead, I heard that Australia was 311 for 2 wickets I wept.' I know the feeling. To experience it, one had to be born to a cricket-worshipping family in the first forty years of this century.

In that milieu, *Wisden* was the necessary bible. One came constantly on secret delights, such as the amazing record of young Master A. E. J.

Collins, who gave us the world's highest recorded innings: 628 not out. Or the longest recorded throw of a cricket ball: 176 yards, hurled by Rev. William Fellowes. Or Albert Trott's famous feat (see above). For all these, *Wisden*, of course, gave the details, in outline at least. It was only years later that I learnt from the indefatigable J. L. Carr that Rev. Fellowes in fact hurled the ball in *anger*, after being jilted by the daughter of the Dean of Christchurch. Or that a luckless youth called Eberle actually dropped Master Collins when he had scored only 20. Or that in 1914, Albert Trott, after making a will on a laundry list, shot himself. I *did* know that he had used a specially commissioned heavy bat, of 3 lb 4 oz. I ordered one myself, when I was at Cambridge, and it ruined what was left of my batting. Anyway, *Wisden* can go only so far. The instinct to hoard this useless information is a mixture of heredity and environment.

I inherited the disease from my father; although I possibly caught it from my elder brother. My father claimed that once in his youth he had actually made over 400, playing against his long-suffering nurse, with a kindly girl as the sole fielder. He retained this devotion all his life, even saying that he wished his ashes to be scattered over the rather bumpy square of school cricket field he laboured to build. Since we were born and brought up in a preparatory school, nets were freely available most of the year, and there was an endless supply of the necessary bats, balls and pads. It was easy to see why we took to the game; but what persuaded my father, the only child of a clergyman and a Scottish girl from Inverawe, to become an addict I do not know. In fact, the high spot of his life, before the Great War, was to play once for his school (Haileybury) at Lord's.

In those days, and until, I think, the 1960s, there used to be, in addition to the Eton and Harrow match, a week of schools cricket at the end of the summer term, in which three pairs of schools (Rugby and Marlborough; Clifton and Tonbridge; and Cheltenham and Haileybury) played two-day matches at Lord's. Until the relentless march of commerce persuaded the authorities that the week had to be dropped on (mainly) financial grounds, ten generations of schoolboys had the chance to step into immaculate flannels, changing in the same dressing rooms used by their heroes Hammond and Bradman, Compton and Edrich, and to step on to the hallowed turf and act out their fantasies. Some of them were decked out in over-handsome blazers and magenta edging, as ours; others in shirts of a delicate duck-egg blue, and so on. The whole experience was one carefully designed to give a small and privileged élite from a small and privileged group of schools a momentary illusion of fame.

For all these reasons, my earliest memories of Lord's were entirely made up of recollections of the schools cricket week; and so was my first introduction to this very magical place. Schools Week was only momentarily eclipsed even by the Second World War (in 1944, I think). This meant that, in order to be present, my brother and I came up to stay for an exciting night or two in the Great Western Hotel at Paddington, or in the fringes of London, quite unmindful of the air raids the Germans sometimes unsportingly arranged for the first week in August. (Once I stayed, I think, in Ruislip, and was disappointed that the guns were too far away.)

My first introduction to these mysteries was as an eleven-year-old in 1941. What I remember about Lord's at that time was mainly the old Tavern, and the leisurely and good-tempered queues for iced coffee and bath buns. I also took a great liking for the scorecards, which were produced constantly through the day, and constantly updated, in a noisy clattering print room beneath the Grandstand, on top of which was fixed the famous Old Father Time weather vane (once pulled from its perch, we were told, by an errant barrage balloon). At that age, my brother and I used to keep the score, in our own scorebooks, throughout the match. The scorecards, memory tells me, cost sixpence. We probably bought three or four each day.

At that time, the two stands on either side of the Pavilion were rather amateur and old-fashioned affairs. The seats were wooden, not concrete as at the other end of the ground, and spattered with elegantly dressed parents. In 1945 we cycled from Hertford to Hendon to stay with a friend, and cycled into Lord's from there. And in the year following, fame came closer. My elder brother Dick was actually playing, which caused my father enormous contentment. In fact, as a very young leg-spinner, he did so well that he was picked for the representative side the week following, having then to bowl at such as David Sheppard and Peter May. I should remember something now about *that*, but I don't. I don't, for instance, even recall any ice-creams being sold, although no doubt the beer was plentiful.

Things from there on seemed specially arranged to please my father.

The next year brother Dick managed to go in late, at number eight, and still made a cheerful 110. (His captain, John Harrison, had been given out earlier by either Beet or Fowler – the umpires were *always* Beet and Fowler – when he had made 99. He made up for it, in the second innings, by making 100 not out; a gesture of magnificent defiance.)

The following year I, too, was playing. I remember arriving at the ground in a cab and walking self-consciously through the gates carrying my cricket bag, beside my brother. Most of the rest is a blur. I recall grandly ordering a drink in the bar behind the Long Room. I remember the lunch (ham and salad, and fruit salad and ice-cream). But, rather oddly, I don't remember going out to bat – in the first innings, at least, in which I made 15 – although I remember marching down the stairs from the balcony, and through the Long Room to the wooden steps that led down to that marvellous spread of gently sloping turf. Brother Dick took a lot of wickets with his leg-spinners and googlies. And in the second innings together we hit off the 90-odd runs necessary to win. Father was, not unnaturally, in his seventh heaven.

The year following, I was on my own. And, by a strange quirk of fate, I, too, was lucky enough to make a hundred, also batting at number eight; just as brother Dick had done two years before. One would think such an experience would be full of memories. Yet, strangely, very little remains. I remember twice driving the opposition opening bowler to the Pavilion rails in the same over to pass 50, and the pleasant rattling sound that made. And I remember, when on 97, making a wild swing outside my off stump at a long-hop, which flew off the shoulder of the bat towards a startled gully and thence down towards the Tavern for four. It should have been caught. Luckily it wasn't: and I can still see the fielder's open mouth.

My father was a contented soul, who, I think, achieved most of his ambitions in life. He often remarked that if he were to have his time over again, he would have liked to have lived all his life in the golden Edwardian years. 'Perhaps you would,' I used to say unkindly, 'but not if you had been born a mill worker in Bolton.' This never riled him. There was a warm sunset glow on his life, for some inner spiritual reason, despite his surviving four years in the trenches, and two unpleasant wounds. All the same, it is nice to think that my brother and I pleased him a lot in his later years by our modest achievements in the one arena he really worshipped: Lord's. It was the high spot of our cricketing career. All that followed afterwards was downhill. Of course it was also very unimportant, even as a minute footnote in cricketing history; but it was fun while it lasted. And visiting Lord's again after so many years still stirs a few memories – notably of the impressive spaces in that great Pavilion, of the broad stairs, the wide passages, and the spacious bar behind the Long Room, and, of course, the Long Room itself..

As I made my way out, the normal life of Lord's out of season continued. In the Library the great E. W. Swanton was to be seen browsing among the topmost leaves in the forest of books like some herbivorous pachyderm. Outside, middle-aged men in dark blue blazers and grey flannels were leaving the Pavilion after an important meeting. I stood on the turf again to take a final look around. Old Father Time and the Grandstand were of course still there; but, like the Pavilion, they seem somehow to have been absorbed into the whole arena, diminishing the importance of those two great buildings which Charlie Cundall had recorded so beautifully half a century ago.

Rain began to fall. Outside the Grace Gates I stood waiting hopefully for a taxi, hatless and coatless. After 10 minutes none had passed. As I continued to wait, I thought of the ghostly voice of W.G. saying, 'We Graces ain't water spaniels' to a friend who asked why he didn't bath after a long innings (they don't tell you *that* kind of thing in the Cricket Memorial Gallery!).

Feeling more and more like a water spaniel, I wondered whether anyone else lamented the passing of that anachronistic Schools Week at Lord's. Did *anyone* still remember it? Schools used to take cricket so fearfully seriously when it all started. Indeed, a headmaster of Eton once flogged the entire school XI, *including* the unfortunate scorer, when they returned from a defeat by Westminster School. There came to be an almost religious element about the rituals they devised: hence those colourful blazers (or robes). Now both rituals and congregations have vanished as though they had never been. Only the temple survives.

Like John Letts, Alan Ross first played at Lord's as a schoolboy. He later played for the same school, Haileybury. Since then he has even written poetry, memoirs and books on cricket as well as being cricket correspondent of the Observer. *Since 1961 he has also edited* The London Magazine.

First Appearances

ALAN ROSS

To play at Lord's is an early and unlikely ambition, and once achieved, unless one turns professional, soon over. Much greater and more prolonged pleasures come from attendance on the celebrated, here at the holiest of cricket grounds most of all. Yet the first pleasure is sweet and, despite disappointment, cannot be discountenanced. In my first match there, at the age of fourteen, not a ball was bowled. My parents came from India, I was photographed with the wrinkled Archie Fowler, then coach at Lord's, and it poured from dawn till dusk. Two years later this non-drama was repeated even more devastatingly, for this was the last summer before the war and it would be six years before I saw my family again. In between whiles, in lovely weather but in circumstances made unreal by war and separation, I made various appearances – for school, university and the Navy – but it was not the same, the original thrill of anticipation curiously muted. Then it was finished for ever, the details indelible because there were so few of them. Cricket at Lord's is one thing; elsewhere quite another.

Next to playing, writing is second-best, but it provided me for twenty-five years with a magical attachment to the game otherwise impossible.

Memory is selective, but when I remember the great moments they are always the same and always at Lord's: Hutton's 145 in 1953, his first match at Lord's as captain against Australia; Dexter's slaughtering of Hall and Griffith in the fantastic drawn Test of 1962, when the game finished with England needing 6 runs and West Indies 1 wicket; the unbelievable salvaging of what seemed a lost cause by Watson and Bailey against Australia in 1953; Weekes's dazzling 90 in 1957, when injured and ill. The images, once started, chase one another like shuffled cards: Colin Bland's fielding in front of the Grandstand; a hook by Colin Milburn into the Tavern; Barnes and Rhodes in their old age sitting together in the sun outside the Pavilion; Sussex winning the first two playings of the Gillette Cup.

Lord's is also about friendship, a kind of staging post in the development of relationships. 'I'll see you at Lord's,' people say to one another. Often they seek out (or avoid) meetings with school friends, business associates, wartime colleagues, whom they never see at any other time.

For years I used to sit in the upper tier of the Pavilion and on Test match days would expect to find behind me Simon Raven and Mark Boxer. Below, the bald pate of the elegantly suited and bow-tied Tom Rosenthal, managing director of Secker & Warburg, publishers, would flush in the sun. On less glamorous occasions Michael Meyer, contemporary at Oxford and biographer-translator of numerous Swedes, could be observed hurrying to or from the tennis court, his red hair glistening. Bernard Gutteridge, eminent soldier-poet and equally eminent toper, would arrive from J. Walter Thompson and talk away sunny afternoons in the Grandstand. Most of all, Jeremy Hutchinson, QC, fresh from defending spies and sinners, and his then wife, Peggy Ashcroft, would be regular companions in the Warner, though more frequently at Hove. We repair old friendships at Lord's, in a way it is impossible to imagine others doing at The Oval or elsewhere.

Not everyone comes to Lord's to watch. Lt Col. G. H. M. 'Buns' Cartwright, who once sent me off the field at Lord's for wearing a torn shirt in a Services match, took latterly to sitting behind the sight-screen, with his back to the play. This was not, like the American novelist Henry James, who did the same at Rye, through an excess of aesthetic sensibility, but as an expression of distaste, fuelled by alcohol, for the modern game.

When I first started writing about cricket for the *Observer* in the early 1950s I used to work in the MCC members' writing room. I had to go elsewhere eventually because C. B. Fry, sycophantic cronies on either side, occupied the front seat and talked incessantly, in dead as well as living languages. Fry was not then quite the grandee of old, and I wish I had known then what I know now about his bizarre marriage and strange existence as nominal commander of the training ship *Mercury*. But he was a maker of phrases – 'Cricket is a dance with a bat in the hand' – and he had style. No one attested to his lordliness better than his one-time secretary, Denzil Batchelor, describing Fry's departure for Lord's: 'The Bentley is at the door; Mr Brooks, the chauffeur, is wisecracking out of the side of his gutta-percha mouth. Aboard are writing pads and binoculars and travelling rugs, a copy of Herodotus, a box of Henry Clay cigars, and reserve hampers of hock and chicken sandwiches in case there has been a strike of caterers in north-west London. A monocle glitters. A silver crest passes, high and haughty, above the cities of the plain. C. B. Fry is off to Lord's.'

That really is the way to arrive for work. There was nothing like it in my day. We had to make do with Swanton's presence, Cardus's anecdotes, Frank Rostron's cigars, Arlott's Rioja, and Bruce Harris's typewriter.

People sometimes remember Lord's for things quite other than cricket. For myself, it was where a love affair began, one which might not have happened had not cricket been a lucky ingredient and shared passion.

John Robert Troutbeck Barclay was another youthful Lord's debutante but, unlike the two previous contributors, went on to become a serious county cricketer, captaining Sussex from 1981 to 1986. He is now Director of Cricket and Coaching at the Arundel Castle Cricket Foundation.

Eton Throw in a Tiddler

J. R. T. BARCLAY

Lord's – was I really going to play on the most famous cricket ground in the world? Me, just a tiddler of barely 5 feet who, earlier in the summer, was playing in the Colts? 'Eton Throw in a Tiddler at Lord's': that was the headline in the *Evening Standard* and now, here I was, sitting on the coach with a team of grown-ups (or so they seemed to me) who would never normally have bothered to speak to me but for cricket. Now we were part of the same team, on our way to Lord's to play against Harrow in the oldest and perhaps most famous fixture played there each year.

Wasn't fate an extraordinary thing? If I hadn't been hit on the foot in the nets back in May I might never have attempted to bowl off-spin at all and then, even if I had, I am not sure that many captains would have had the nerve to give me a bowl in the first Colts match of the season. But here I made full use of the privilege of captaincy and brought myself on to bowl first change and to everybody's surprise took six wickets, never suspecting that the Eton captain, yes, the Eton First XI captain, was actually searching for a spin-bowler and had his spies out. He must have been desperate because, despite my age – just 14½ – and size, I was given a chance and soon found that older batsmen, too, could be fooled by slow flighted deliveries.

We were now approaching London. I had only been to Lord's once before on the occasion of Sussex's great triumph in the first Gillette

ETON XI

Cup final five years earlier in 1963. I had vivid memories of sitting on the grass in front of the Nursery stands with my godfather and elder brother, by far the best place from which to appreciate the mystery and splendour of the great Pavilion and watch the heads of incoming batsmen bobbing between members in the Long Room before bravely descending the steps on to the field. I remembered the crowd's excited hush as we awaited Dexter's arrival: silence erupted into a wild ovation as he strode imperiously on to the ground. Ten minutes later a chill passed through the Sussex supporters when Gifford had him caught at slip for only 3. For me this was the ultimate catastrophe and I was convinced that Sussex could not possibly recover from such a devastating blow. A total of 168 was surely not enough, but the Worcester batting was gradually worn down by some relentlessly accurate Sussex bowling. Rain began to fall quite heavily, but nobody moved. Dexter at one stage placed every fielder on the boundary until finally, in the penultimate over and amidst ecstatic excitement, Bob Carter, Worcestershire's last batsman, was run out and Sussex had won by 14 runs. A day to remember.

I observed from the coach window that the street signs had NW8 on them so I knew we must be getting near and before my mind had time to wander again the coach swept into the ground. We were there.

With aching right arm I dragged my cricket bag into the Pavilion, which consisted of vast staircases and long corridors all smelling slightly of rubber. Bumping my way along, eventually I found the Home Team dressing room which for some reason was allocated to Eton. The room was enormous but I spotted a quiet corner, dumped my bag down, and collapsed exhausted on to a chair. Already I seemed to have walked miles and couldn't imagine how I would ever find my way from the dressing room to the wicket. As I looked round my eyes fell upon several cricket cases neatly stowed away under lockers: F. J. Titmus; P. H. Parfitt; W. E. Russell; J. T. Murray – heroes indeed! I had all their signatures in my autograph book, acquired after waiting for hours behind the pavilion at Hove. A favourite game was to trade autographs – a Titmus, a Parfitt, a Murray and two Russells for a Dexter, who was always the ultimate conquest. Now here I was surrounded by names from my autograph book. I decided that I would sit next to Titmus's case as I knew he bowled off-spinners and hoped that some of his magic might rub off on me.

Oddly enough, I must have been so immersed in the prospect of the match ahead that I remember little of the immediate build-up, except that a huge wave of relief struck me when I heard that we had won the toss and elected to bat. At least I was spared any instant activity and made the most of this respite by hungrily tucking into a splendid assortment of biscuits wheeled in on a huge trolley.

The match started, but within 2 overs my appetite deserted me: both opening batsmen out for 0, and already I wondered when the number eleven batsman should pad up without affecting team morale. I need not have worried because Faber and Cazalet, our most consistent batsmen, quickly repaired the damage and with some fast scoring added 126 for the third wicket. But it was too good to last and as soon as Coomaraswamy, Harrow's captain and left-arm spin-bowler, broke through, the collapse was swift. When Faber finally departed for a brilliant century I decided to prepare for batting.

Suitably protected I sat on the balcony, very silent, and surveyed the scene. There was a lot of noise and sporadic chanting created by groups of rival supporters returning from sumptuous picnic lunches, while the cricket, oblivious to all this, remained intense. The atmosphere did nothing to soothe me as I waited anxiously for the ninth wicket to fall. Inevitably the moment came: Tomkin was batting at the time, and very well too, when suddenly he chanced his arm once too often, rushed down the wicket, missed the ball and was stumped. With a lump in my throat I picked up my bat and gloves and hurried to the dressing-room door, so great was my concern to reach the wicket in good time. Down the giant staircase I went and into the Long Room, which seemed to be full of old men staring at me, and I wondered whether the crowd at the Nursery End would now be able to see *my* head bobbing up and down between the members as I made my way to the great door which led on to the field. Probably not, I thought; I was a bit small.

When I got outside it was very noisy – some abuse, I expect, but also words of encouragement, and I couldn't help remembering the Dexter ovation as I walked as fast as I dared to the middle, ignoring the cold stares of the opposition. At last I reached the crease and looked at the umpire. 'Middle and leg, please,' I tried to say, but no more than an inaudible squeak came out. 'You've got centre there,' the umpire answered kindly, which I acknowledged by banging the ground to mark my guard. I did not deem it important at this critical moment to be too particular about what guard I took. I looked around me and observed almost every fielder closing in on me intimidatingly and clearly not expecting me to last long. Meanwhile, Coomaraswamy was spinning the ball fiendishly from hand to hand and I dared not look at him for fear of being mesmerized. I took my stance, 'play,' said the umpire, and Coomaraswamy trotted in and released the ball. As he did so, and without for one moment watching to see where the ball might be travelling, I thrust out my left leg and bat. There then followed the most joyous of sensations as, simultaneously, I heard and felt a heart-warming clonk as the ball by chance collided with my bat. Despite my paralytic fear I had now hit a ball at Lord's. 'Over,' said the umpire. I stepped away from the stumps and with great pride gazed up at the Grandstand scoreboard to confirm my score – 0 NOT OUT – and for a second or two I didn't feel anyone could ever have wished for more from life.

Andrew Douglas-Home, my partner at the other end, and I were determined to show that we could bat better than our positions in the order suggested. Sadly, the third ball of the next over was straight, Andrew missed it and we were all out for 210, Barclay 0 not out. What an achievement! I was so pleased both to hit one and remain undefeated. There may have been many more distinguished 0 not outs played at Lord's, but surely none that meant so much. I strode off amidst great applause although I was well aware that it was not directed at me but at the Harrow captain whose marvellous bowling produced figures of 7 for 42.

Harrow began their innings badly, losing an early wicket, and it wasn't until after tea that they settled down. It was then that I sensed I would soon be called upon to bowl. The summons duly came: 'Next over that end.' I tried to look confident but the only thing likely to spin was my head: would I ever pitch it, bowl it straight and spin it, simultaneously? Indeed, would I be able to release the ball at all? These were the horrors that began to overwhelm me while Douglas-Home bowled from the other end. 'Over,' said the umpire at long last. There was no escape now; it was my turn. In the circumstances Kinkead-Weekes was the ideal captain, calm and quiet, and came to my rescue as I prepared to bowl. While I marked out my short run he spread the fielders out sympathetically, appreciating that I had to bowl at Webster, the Harrow opening batsman, who was already in full flow. Play. I scuttled up to the wicket and hurriedly released the ball, a full toss on the leg stump. Webster's bat swung elegantly and cracked the ball past mid-on for four. How I got through that over I shall never know, but somehow I did and only conceded 7 runs. Slowly I found some rhythm, but so did the Harrow batsmen who, for a long time, were completely untroubled; until suddenly and without warning, as the Grandstand shadows began to stretch across the ground, I bowled an innocent half-volley to Harrison, Webster's hard-hitting left-handed partner. He whacked it hard and low and I turned just in time to watch mid-on tumble to his left and cling on to a fine catch. A wicket at last, a wicket at Lord's; not my best ball but what did that matter.

It was nearing close of play now and with Webster fast approaching his century the ball was tossed to me to bowl the final over. The first five balls were played with the disciplined straight bat of a man determined to reach three figures the next day. 'I'll try a swinger,' I thought, as I walked back to bowl the last ball and rubbed the ball vigorously on my flannels. The swinger was a ball I was learning to bowl as a variation from the off-break although I had not yet mastered the art of disguising it. Surely the mighty Webster was bound to spot it? Anyway, I bowled the ball and it began to drift gently away down the hill towards slip, enticing the cautious batsman forward to consider this tempting morsel. Webster continued to follow the ball as a salmon might a fly and against his better instinct went for it with a full flourish, expecting, I am sure, to end the day on a grand note. But it was not to be and instead of a glorious stroke the ball just nibbled the outside edge of his bat and flew to Cazalet at slip who snapped up the chance. It was a wonderful way to end my first day's cricket at Lord's.

The following morning Harrow continued to score freely and it was not long before they passed our total. Naturally, I was the target for much of this aggression, but the batsmen had to take risks in the process. I was lucky to be bowling still and had my captain to thank for maintaining faith in me despite the onslaught. Harrow were finally all out for 260, a lead of 50, and I finished with 6 for 100 and was allowed to lead the team off the field for the first time in my life – at Lord's.

Confronted with this deficit the match deteriorated quickly for Eton and the two crucial blows came when Cazalet and Faber were dismissed in quick succession after lunch, Faber to a miraculous catch at backward short leg by Webster from a full-blooded hook, and Cazalet lbw. We never recovered from this and soon Coomaraswamy was bamboozling us again with his destructive spin. In this second innings I was surprisingly promoted to number nine – a slight mystery; surely my 0 not out had not been that impressive? Once again I did not have to wait long before I was on my way down those stairs, through the Long Room and down the steps to see if I could improve upon my first innings.

The ground became very noisy, mainly with chanting Harrovians cheering their team on to victory. The challenge ahead was awesome but I was determined to keep my nerve. 'Get forward, whatever you do, left leg down the wicket,' Vic Cannings, the Eton coach, impressed upon me vigorously before I left the Pavilion. Surrounded by blue-and-white-stripe-capped fielders I took guard, watched the ball (so I thought), and stepped back only to hear the ball fizz past me and strike the middle stump with a sickening clunk. Out first ball, 122 for 8. Disaster, and I had such high hopes of steering the team to safety, but now, in an instant, these were dashed and amidst the uproar I was trudging, sad and lonely, with nowhere to hide, back to the Pavilion. Why did I go back to it? I had meant to go forward. Yet another unsolved cricketing mystery. What would Vic say? Back in the dressing room it was very quiet, an atmosphere of hushed and uncomfortable tension with which I was to become most familiar in the years to come.

The match didn't last much longer and finally we subsided for 141. Coomaraswamy was Harrow's hero, too good for us, and took 5 for 50 to give him the admirable match figures of 12 for 92. It left Harrow needing just 92 to win, which was achieved comfortably enough for the loss of only three wickets. Despite the disappointment, there was still time to savour the extraordinary atmosphere before finally trotting up the Pavilion steps knowing full well that I might never play at Lord's again.

In fact, I did play again, many times, but nothing could ever match the vivid impression of that first experience.

. If I have a single favourite piece of Lord's prose it is probably the essay by R. C. Robertson-Glasgow, who bowled for Somerset and then became the Observer's *cricket correspondent. I was at least half-inclined to include it here alongside the offering from his direct descendant, Vic Marks, also a Somerset cricketer of distinction (he bowled slower than 'Crusoe' but, unlike him, captained the county), and, since 1989, also the* Observer's *cricket correspondent.*

Too Many Stuffed Shirts

VIC MARKS

The introduction of the Gillette Cup in 1963 opened the gates of Lord's to a new brand of spectator. County stalwarts from the provinces, who would not have dreamt of attending a Test match, now determined to make an expedition up to London to support their local heroes. Doggedly they braved the traffic or the tube as well as the gatemen, and like intruders at a royal garden party took their seats along with MCC members. The plebeian cricket-lover encroached upon a world which he had supposed to be the sole domain of the privileged male – Lord's Cricket Ground.

In 1967 Somerset reached the final and my father and I, having put our faith in British Rail and London Transport, were, of course, relieved to claim our seats underneath Old Father Time at 10.30. Our elation was short-lived as Denness and Luckhurst flayed the luckless Somerset attack all around Lord's. Unfortunately, we were not the only ones overawed by the occasion and the scoreboard registered 129 for 1 at lunch. After the interval Somerset rallied bravely and so did their supporters. One group, clad in smocks and sucking straw – just to strengthen the Londoners' misconception of West Country life – had decided to down a pint of scrumpy at the capture of every Kent wicket.

Within 90 minutes nine wickets fell, so that after a morning of almost complete abstinence their stamina was sorely tested.

Now even the sober had cause for optimism; we needed just 194 for victory, but that was too many. Up on the balcony Colin Cowdrey politely raised the Cup and the two of us were so drained and disappointed that we left our sandwich bag at St John's Wood tube station.

Eleven years later my father was in the stands again and Somerset were overawed again; but this time I was in the dressing room. We still felt like foreigners; there were too many starched shirts and local rules. Setting out down the staircase to bat I had to weave through several members who were clearly more intent upon having a pee than witnessing my impending innings. They didn't seem to realize that this could be my finest hour. Ten minutes later, as I trudged back through the Long Room, the silence was deafening. From their high perches they all just looked at me, or rather looked down on me, like High Court judges. Some uncomplicated West Country abuse would have been infinitely preferable.

We counter-attacked the following year (1979) by rebelling a little. It wasn't a conscious decision, yet the Somerset players were easily recognizable as they entered the Pavilion, jeans and T-shirts contrasting vividly with all the three-piece suits and red and yellow ties. Those notices requiring – not requesting – everyone practising at the Nursery End to wear whites prompted everyone to pack their blue tracksuit bottoms. We were grimly determined to make ourselves at home even if the gatemen didn't recognize most of us until they had perused the names on our sponsored cars.

We won and gloried in the balcony scene, proudly collecting our medals and then lingering there – kings for a day – to wave to the thousands congregated below.

Thereafter Lord's no longer intimidated us. Viv Richards came to regard this ground as the best possible venue to parade his talents; it was his favourite stage. We learnt to exploit the oddities of the ground rather than fear them. Joel Garner hurtled in from the Pavilion End and disconsolate batsmen would later inform us that the ball would emanate not from the sight-screen but from the murky windows of that matchless Pavilion. Botham eyed the Tavern boundary hungrily, acknowledging Newton's discovery that cricket balls travel faster

downhill. The same principle applied to my off-spinners. I bowled at the 'wrong' end, the Nursery End, attempting to compel the batsman to hit the ball up the slope where all the whippets were stationed.

Sometimes the enormity of the occasion could be exploited. Innocuous off-spinners generously flighted, which on a Sunday at Taunton were destined for the River Tone, might here be treated with undue reverence. No batsman likes to fail in the final so, mistakenly, he might adopt a no-risk policy, rejecting the idea of lofted drives, but choosing instead to wait for rubbish; the slower the ball was propelled the harder it became to penetrate the infield with low-risk nudges and deflections.

We developed a happy routine for finals – a rare team dinner on the Friday night during which we consumed one glass of port too many to ensure a good night's sleep. There was a ritual discussion of the match: invariably we decided that every opposition batsman was vulnerable to the bowling of Garner, conveniently forgetting that he had only 12 overs at his disposal; we might spend 20 minutes discussing Randall's bowling or Kevin Jarvis's batting. In fact, few of our observations bore any relation to what happened the following day, but we all went to bed happy, content to dwell upon the possibility of victory rather than all the mistakes we might make.

So by 1983 Somerset players and spectators felt comfortable at Lord's. This time it was Kent who needed 194 for victory, but it was too many. Up on the balcony Ian Botham raised the Cup to the masses below a little less sheepishly than Colin Cowdrey sixteen years before, and my father's sandwich bag accompanied him all the way home.

Mike Selvey is an appropriate partner for Vic Marks. He, too, played county cricket (for Middlesex) and reports on the game for a national paper (The Guardian). Like his fellow Middlesex fast bowler, J. J. Warr, he has pronounced views on the Lord's gatemen.

'Morning, Mike'

MIKE SELVEY

I was up at Lord's, me and a couple of hundred others. It was only an ordinary county match and nothing to get excited about. But there was something funny going on. As I passed through the Grace Gates, the gateman gave me a cheery wave. Puzzled, I responded in kind. As I made my way towards the entrance to the press box, at the back of the Warner Stand, I sauntered past the attendant by the Pavilion door. 'Morning, Mike, how are you?' There's definitely something afoot, I thought. It took a while to realize what it was but suddenly it hit me. I had finally been accepted at Headquarters as a non-cricketer. Perhaps, if I rolled back the years, I could better explain what I mean.

It is a glorious sunny day in early June and the crowds are already milling along the St John's Wood Road, chattering animatedly as they make their way towards the Grace Gates. It is Test match day: which one exactly I can't remember now. A white Jaguar noses noiselessly past cabs dropping members off, and pulls up at the gates. The occupant, blond, 6 ft 8 in tall, and pretty recognizable in these parts, waits patiently for the gates to swing open and admit him. He waits in vain until at last they open a crack and an elderly gent walks out and peers myopically into the car. The driver pushes a button and the window hisses down. 'Can I see your pass, sir?' asks the old man. The only thing that Tony Greig could do was laugh. He might as well have done; everyone else did. 'Sorry, I haven't got one,' he replied. 'Well, you can't

come in here, then,' the England captain was told, and the man shambled back inside and closed the gates once more.

Anyway, I digress, so back to the rear door. This time it's only a county match so there aren't too many people about. (Cricket and people only interfere with the smooth running of the place anyway, Mike Smith, a Grade A, kite-marked cynic, used to say.) A distinguished silver-haired gentleman appears from the path between the Memorial Rose Garden and the Middlesex office and makes his way to the door. He receives the same greeting as Greig. 'Can I see your pass, sir?' 'I'm sorry,' replies the gent, 'I've left it at home.' 'Then I'm afraid you can't come in here,' he is told. 'Oh, dear,' says the gentleman. 'I'll just have to use my own key then, won't I?' and with that Gubby Allen toddled off down to the other rear door and let himself into the building.

Now the point of these tales is to show that if those two, both megastars at HQ in their different ways, couldn't get into the place, what hope is there for the rest of us? The short answer is none. I suffered any number of indignities. Once, like Greig, I was refused entry to the ground on the morning of a big match, a cup semi-final maybe, by someone to whom I had passed pleasantries on probably half the summers' mornings for the previous ten years.

On another occasion, a policeman actually reached in through my car window during an inquisition at the gate and confiscated my keys to prevent me getting further. I was forced to abandon ship in the forecourt. And like Gubby Allen I was not allowed into the Pavilion once 'because Middlesex aren't at home today'. I would not have minded so much if it had been a Test or something, but it was 4 January, the snow lay thick on the ground, and I had only called in while passing to wish people a Happy New Year.

It would be wrong of me, however, to convey the impression that this antagonism was in any way unilateral. When I was a player we (all right, I) did not help the cause by flaunting as many rules as possible. So Pavilion attendants who spent their lives turning away anyone not sporting the requisite tie and tweeds had to bite their tongues and admit an assortment of old T-shirts, vests, jeans and pumps. In any other era but the Brearley one it would not have worked; with him it did, largely because he was as badly turned out as anyone. Once we convened a 'Bad Taste Day' when the whole team was expected to arrive for the match so appallingly dressed as to defy description. The success of the venture was marred only when the team physiotherapist, John Miller, was unanimously voted the winner: he was not even aware there had been a competition. This was the same Miller, incidentally, who, blind as a bat, once strapped up a bowler's injured thigh and, when finished, while the bowler nearly gave himself a hernia suppressing the laughter, carefully snipped through both the end of the bandage and his tie which had got caught in the strapping.

Playing cricket at Lord's had, in spite of the drawbacks, or perhaps because of them, a certain magic, even when there was no one in the ground. There was the dressing room, for instance. When I first joined Middlesex in 1972 the room was hierarchical, but cosy. There were a number of old sofas and, in the corners either side of the French windows onto the balcony, two dressing tables. Mike Smith used one to change by, with an armchair of contemporary design to sit in. He was the team's representative on the Players' Association committee, and the mirror became the noticeboard with letters offering winter jobs abroad or travel arrangements for the next away match pinned on the frame for scrutiny. Brearley had the other dressing table, but his armchair was an antique leather affair. Next to that was a huge throne-like thing, also leather, which was first occupied by John Price and then on his retirement bequeathed to me. It was a marvellous slumping chair after a day in the field. The rest of the room contained two massive tables in the middle, a physio's couch with his lamps and machinery next to it, wooden chairs under pegs alongside one wall, a row of washbasins by the other, and along the back, the lockers, awarded according to seniority.

Alas, it changed. One day we came in to find our comfortable old stuff removed and steel and green leatherette benches, in the style of second-class continental railway carriages, fitted round the walls. The armchairs went into the basement where, as far as I know, they remain to this day, and the physio was allocated a room to himself.

Always fussing about in the background, whistling tunelessly, was Roy Harrington, the dressing-room attendant who, among his many qualities, had an unrivalled knack of producing the morning tea while we were at practice, so that on our return it tasted of old socks (and some of the socks were bad – Bill Merry's cricket socks once set off a bomb detector at Dublin airport, but that's another story).

After play, there were the biggest, deepest baths in the cricket world, gentlemen's baths, with the ever present sack of soda crystals to soften the water, huge shower-heads, which had they ever been descaled would have sluiced down like Niagara, and oodles of hot water, even though MCC had an extraordinary ability to synchronize the annual overhaul of the boilers with pre-season training and nets.

There was the corporate clump out to play, down the stairs to the Long Room, past pictures that no one ever noticed – I once took a straw poll on what they were, and not one person could nominate a single painting or print, except the one, by Gubby's back door, of a top-hatted bloke in fingerless gloves and sitting in a bathchair. One player even insisted that he went past a particular large portrait every day until he was shown the same picture at The Oval later in the season. For county games we would trail through the silence of the Long Room, often starting our own applause. On big matches it was different – then it was a squeeze even to get through, and if you did well the plaudits echoed to the ceiling. If you'd got a first-baller though, the silence could be deafening.

I missed all these things when I retired from the game, and many more: Miller's tales (there was not very much going on in the confines of Lord's that he didn't know about); dressing-room banter with the wit barbed and biting but rarely malicious; Nancy's lunches, reckoned to be the best in the business (good place to get rained off, Lord's). And stuffy old MCC, of course. But I had memories of what they could be like, favourite tales, like the dressing-room driving range. One rainy day, with nothing better to do, a contest was devised to see who could drive a golf ball the furthest from the middle of the dressing room, through the open French windows 10 feet away and on to the middle of the square, a test not only of strength, but accuracy. As the only available set of clubs were left-handed, entry was severely limited – to Ian Gould, in fact. Nevertheless, gamely, he decided to have a go. With the rest of the team barricaded behind the up-turned tables, he teed up, on an inverted hairbrush, and proceeded to drill shots superbly on to the square. Unfortunately, this coincided with a pitch inspection and neither umpires nor groundsman took too kindly to the intervention. Nor did the MCC Secretariat. An official stormed along and enquired what the devil we thought we were playing at and whether Gould (he had been shopped by a team-mate – no names, no extra nets, but the word 'Branston' has a bearing) could explain why he was damaging the Test wicket, which was under preparation. He was not best pleased when Gould confessed to a heavy slice and could the Secretariat recommend a change of grip to direct his shots on to the county pitch where he had been aiming.

Now Lord's for me is a different world; one I never knew or even appreciated existed. Can, for example, these gatemen and attendants, salts of the earth to a man, I now realize, be the same ones who barred the way before; the ones we believed were descended from an élite defence that would have stifled a wartime invasion before it could have begun? 'Have you got your pass, Mr Hitler? Well, I'm sorry, you can't come in here.' Well, of course they are; the players tell me so. The ground may change – its new stands, rebuilt offices, and decent beer in the Long Room bar – but the people haven't. It was just our attitudes as players. It's me that's changed, damn it. When I go to Lord's now, it's in a jacket and with a collar and tie – socks even. No matter how hard I try, for better or for worse, I've joined the Establishment. I even quite like MCC, and what is worse, they quite like me. By God, if I were sixty years younger I might even put my name down.

MCC members of a conventional cast of mind probably shouldn't have read the previous entry, nor, perhaps, should they read the following one. Frank Keating, the sporting essayist of Punch *and* The Guardian *fame, is a cricket enthusiast to his fingertips, but he is ambivalent about cricket HQ. Never mind. Dissent is essential in a free society, even – perhaps* particularly *– when celebrating. And Lord's and MCC are big enough to take it. Well, aren't they?*

Those Gatemen Again

FRANK KEATING

Sorry and all that, but I cannot put my hand on my heart and say I have ever felt totally relaxed at Lord's – and certainly not lollingly, belchingly *comfortable*.

Awe-struck is more the word. Once or twice, sure, in wonder, when I think I've seen the light – but more often in an apprehensive way: uneasy, furtive, and tip-toe trespassing. It is probably those guilt-inducing grey gatemen in grey macs who seem to have been patrolling each entrance to the ground for aeons. All that's missing, I sometimes think, is the Armalite on their shoulder as their narrow eyes greyly flicker from my face to the ticket, like Tijuana border-guards willing themselves to make their day by finding a forged passport at the last check out of Mexico on the highway north to San Diego and the rich life.

My fault, I'm sure. Though I bet a lot of Ovaltineys from way down south in London feel the same.

Once into Lord's, as you queue for a scorecard or evening paper to see how the trenchant tabloid toff, Thicknesse, views the day, you still fear a tap on the shoulder – and the old armlock march away, at the double, through that low-hung, thick, servants' door at the back of the Pavilion and down the cellar steps for interrogation in the same cubicle

deep in the bowels of the members' basement bog in which they pad-
locked Tinniswood's raging brigadier on the occasion of the tie-pulling
riot in the clamorously bellowing afternoon of the Centenary Test.

In fact, I have to admit, they are only old friends who have, so far,
tapped me on the shoulder at Lord's. Old cricketing mates, or boozing
buddies, or former lovers, or distant cousins: and you're delighted to
see them, and catch up on gossip and golly! and gosh! is that so? And
even have a plastic-beakered slurp together at the terrible tat they
turned the Tavern into. Then settle down to watch the cricket – and if
it's a house-full day at a Test match or a grand one-dayer, and the sun's
in its shirtsleeves on high over Trott's turret, and the cricket down there
is gripping and tangy and taut, well, then, fair-do's, Lord's can fully
deserve the ultimate hurrahs for social and sporting resplendence.

I don't go into the press box as much as I should. There you are per-
ched high on the swish rim of the Warner Stand. Too far away, and
everyone positively winces with hate when you ask for a quick dekko
through their binoculars. Not that even the most powerful Japanese
jobs help you to see much that matters from half a mile above deep fine
leg's head. The know-alls cannot remotely twig the deviation in any
delivery from up there – that's probably why, next morning, you read
only that dismissals were caused by 'movement down the hill'. Or
occasionally 'up', by way of balanced, but still oblivious, variation. But
the press box is a good place to make a few free phone calls – and to
have a drink out of a decent glass (i.e., one actually made of the stuff),
invariably served with a smile, too, by Peter or his wife, who could well
be the only duo on the Lord's staff, from those gatemen to the gaffer
himself, with an innate, unselfconscious, and inborn sense of public
relations, generosity of spirits, and the general good-eggness of life
itself.

The very reasons, I suppose, why I've always been more of an Oval
man myself. Been going there longer, see. As a kid I was allowed up to
London for a few days each year, from the dear and dozy West
Country, to stay with Auntie Jo, who kept a boarding house in Pimlico,
on the Embankment. In 1951, Festival of Britain year, I turned right
one Saturday morning, over Vauxhall Bridge, and followed the scurry-
ing throng under the sooty clang and rumble beneath the railway
arches – and into Surrey; and The Oval. The final Test, England against
South Africa. I was entranced.

Hutton was out for *obstructing the field* (involuntarily dabbing at a popping ball, thinking it might be 'played on', which the wicket-keeper, Endean, was moving forward to catch). Then Freddie Brown hoicked a beefily skimming one-bounce four backward of square that would have hit me, I swear, if my neighbour hadn't daringly fielded it with his great big calloused Cockney right mitt. And Peter May got a first-ball duck – which made me warmly, smirkingly glad, because he was keeping my beloved young home-town hero, Graveney, out of the England side. Funny, never had anything but a cold-fish regard for May ever since.

Anyway, point is, the welcoming, worldly, jingle-jangle and *jabber* of The Oval remains, to my mind, a better introduction to big-time cricket than the pontifical, cathedral awe and hush-in-the-close that stately Lord's can induce.

Dickens's *second* choice was Lord's. He was an Ovaltiney; so was Arnold Bennett, and Priestley when Yorkshire came down. Wodehouse and Travers were two who flocked over the river with the 'grandma's funeral, day-off' congregation of errand-boys from the City to see Jessop's innings in 1902.

Just over a hundred years ago, the Rev. James Pycroft defined the Londoners' cricket watching. I fancy it still holds good. The spot-on old Rev. quilled the qualification: 'At The Oval, men seem to have rushed away with some zest and vigour from their City offices. At Lord's all remains languid, and there is a dilettante look as of men whose work and toil, if any, is still to come.'

Cardus, towards the end, preferred Lord's. But then he lived, in his pomp, in Baker Street. In his early days of *greeny-yaller* he wrote of The Oval's atmosphere as 'concentrated and characteristic and Cockney . . . and while the Pavilion at Lord's might be the embodiment of high-minded, select, and ancient authority, so is the gasometer at Kennington the very image of London's friendliness, and its plain and tangible humours.'

Later, he was to deliberate on the difference between London's two grand amphitheatres of, and for, the game of games. It was in his favourite Baker Street steakhouse – 'sirloin, well done; baked potato and parsley butter, please' – just a matter of months before he died in 1975: 'Only, ever, my boy, go the democratic way to The Oval. By bus. Alas, it is no longer possible for you to proceed to Lord's in the proper

and correct manner. That is – by hansom cab. They have become scarce in the land.'

Only Lord's, I'm afraid, could have been so insufferably stuffy and prim (and gormlessly overstruck by the very awe that it perpetrates for itself) to have allowed that calamity on 30 August 1980, the Saturday of the Centenary Test, when a patch of damp grass, a couple of feet square and way off the playing pitch, was dopily deemed dangerous enough to hold up play on a glorious summer's day, for hour upon wretched hour. At The Oval a few years before, we had all been allowed (no, positively encouraged) to troop on and mop up a veritable Noah-like flood with our jumpers and woollies and travelling rugs – so a Test match could restart.

Never at Lord's. Those grey gatemen, for a start, would have a fit.

Surprisingly few contributors have chosen to remember particular matches. The following two who did are both well-known thriller writers, which may be a clue. Or, there again, may not. Allen Synge once hit J. C. Boucher of the Gentlemen of Ireland for consecutive fours, one immediately before and the other immediately after a very Irish lunch. This was no mean achievement as Boucher topped the 1948 first-class bowling averages. Unfortunately, Synge was bowled next ball. He still captains a South London team called The Spies, composed almost entirely of younger relations.

'Everyone Suddenly Burst Out Hitting'

ALLEN SYNGE

We don't know quite how lucky we are. We are fifteen years old with a lifetime of unsuspected peace and cricket before us. God is in His heaven. The war is over in Europe and will soon be officially ended in Asia. What's more, we have arrived only a little late for the third day of England *v* The Dominions at Lord's on 28 August 1945, an encounter the like of which is, for a variety of reasons, unlikely to be seen again.

The sun is shining. The ground is almost full. Yet we can't fully appreciate our good fortune. For instance, we are unaware that this stylish left-hander, batting in a club cap of hornet tail colours, is the future legend, M. P. Donnelly of New Zealand. Nor have we any certain way of knowing that his tousled-haired partner, Flight Lieutenant K. R. Miller, who admittedly had been seen to deal harshly with England's bowling in the recent 'Victory Tests', is about to play the innings of a lifetime. We miss another crucial cause for eager anticipation, simply for lack of historical foresight. This is the fact that England's attack is spearheaded by no less than two leg-spinners,

D. V. P. Wright and E. Hollies. What on earth would the selectors of the second half of this century have said!

Many times since, at the scorecard booth, a shout has gone up – for a near run-out, perhaps, or a fumbled piece of fielding – which has made us hurry to the gap between the Pavilion and Q Stand. But today we have been greeted by extraordinary sounds, as if riflemen were at target practice in the middle of a roaring football stadium. A kind of Bisley gone wild! The simple explanation is that Donnelly and Miller have decided to throw a VJ Day celebration entirely off their own bats, and the spin of Wright and Hollies is doing little to restrain them.

We take our seats in the topmost perch of the Pavilion (there seemed to be no red tape about fathers introducing sons in those days), and all too soon M. P. Donnelly's hornet tail cap disappears under our noses into the Pavilion. A pity, in a way, because there has been some talk of the New Zealander repeating the superb century he made on Saturday. But we can't be too downcast, for now a still perky forty-two-year-old Learie Constantine is making his way to the crease, a name that used to be murmured in the same breath as Bradman and Hitler in one's pre-war infancy.

Miller is looking for historic opportunities in the deep mid-off and mid-on areas, the former a clearable single-tiered stand which the Warner has long since replaced. But Constantine is aiming for sixes all round the clock. One whirling heave nearly takes the head off England's wicket-keeper, S. C. Griffith. My father assures me that the Sussex 'keeper would have faced worse danger as a lieutenant colonel in last year's Arnhem operation.

Yet it's bomber pilot Miller who continues to make the major impact on this spectator, soon very nearly literally. For him England now have five men guarding the Pavilion End pickets; but they might as well be midgets. An off-drive bounds into the pre-Warner stand like a weight-less kangaroo. Then an on-side blow gatecrashes the sociabilities of members and friends in Q Stand. Now Miller takes a swing at the slow-to medium-pacer J. G. W. Davies, shifting his weight only slightly on to the back foot, and suddenly in this Pavilion eyrie one is face to face with a battered ball which, again as luck will have it, is still airborne. It smacks into the roofing overhead while a few rows below BBC commentators and technicians are yanked from their seats, spilling cigarette ash down their double-breasted demob suits and swearing like troopers. Flight

Lieutenant Miller has missed Alfred Trott's total Pavilion clearance by a few tiles! The ball, we understand, is finally retrieved from the vicinity of the tennis court building and presented with all due ceremony at the Pavilion door for return to the field of play.

Almost certainly the untoward fireworks of the England *v* The Dominions match were the result of a conspiracy. There can be little doubt that the Lord's authorities and the players of both sides had conspired to mount a dazzling shop window for restored first-class cricket in the three-day context, notwithstanding the fact that the ground was still grey from wartime neglect, and in the Long Bar men in tired suits queued for tea and raisin cake as if both commodities were rationed. The authorities were as lucky as the spectators to be able to call upon so many Dominions players (no talk of Commonwealth just then) whom the fortunes of war had deposited in England. Only the skipper Constantine, and he only for reasons of age, was a fully fledged civilian. Uniforms were as common as blazers in the changing-rooms one was unaccountably allowed to blunder into. But now that the war was shortly due to be wrapped up at a ceremony on board the USS *Missouri* in Tokyo harbour, the coats were coming off in the battle for 'brighter cricket', one of the ringing watchwords of the post-war era.

Perhaps the expectations raised by this amazing if quaintly named game weren't quite fulfilled in after years; but then when the Government was forced to introduce bread rationing in 1947 the whole nation began to feel that peace had been a bit of a let-down. True, we would have the wonderful Compton and Edrich season, and Miller would visit Lord's several times again. Yet all too often we would watch England grimly hanging on against Australia and West Indies and, later, weaker Commonwealth (now if you please) sides rendered strokeless against England's increasing pace-bowling resources. Again, fewer and fewer of the myriad faces that beamed into one's borrowed binoculars like sunflowers that August afternoon would pass through the turnstiles for county games.

Meanwhile, Doug Wright, with a run-up that would exhaust a modern pace-bowler, and Eric Hollies, of the shorter to the wicket shuffle, are demonstrating that while leg-spinners can be hit they can also neatly demolish a tail. Miller goes, caught by a staggering James Langridge at deep mid-off from Wright's bowling, for 185 (he has put on a hundred in 75 minutes!), and the last four Dominions wickets fall for the addition of 6 scored runs. It's now after lunch on the final day and England need 357 to win. Hammond has no hesitation in going for them.

Afterwards *The Cricketer* would pray in print that 'the scientists who apparently in these days can do anything would invent some kind of gland that would enable Hammond to go on playing for another 10 years!' Certainly, in an unaging world one fancies Hammond would always be England's captain. The sheer dignity of his stance at first slip alone defied any thoughts of a likely successor. Now, with Fishlock, Robertson and Langridge dismissed cheaply, Walter Hammond decides to teach the wild colonial boy Miller a lesson in controlled hitting. Without any seeming exertion he starts to find the mid-off and mid-on fences. Then, with no discernible power acceleration, he begins to hit sixes. No mighty heaves. Hammond's sixes are a natural extension of a straight swing and solid footwork. One such boundary leaper pulls up just short of the reaching hands of players on the England balcony and falls among ducking members on the Pavilion terrace. 'Everyone suddenly burst out singing,' the poet Siegfried Sassoon wrote on the merciful conclusion of the First World War. Here at Lord's in August 1945 everyone suddenly burst out hitting.

Eyes that had watched London burning, seen V-bombs diving, and had, no doubt, gazed on the horrors of battlefield war were feasting on this scene. For myself, who had spent a largely inglorious war as an evacuee in the United States, the game was also a revelation. During a three and a half year spell in the vast territories of the unconverted, it had become increasingly difficult to defend, or explain, a passion for cricket, since my experience of the big occasion was limited to an afternoon at the Eton and Harrow match in 1939, which as it happened had coincided with the riotous celebrations that attended Harrow's first victory over the old rival since 1908. To the charge of my American school pals that cricket was a monumentally boring game, I had invariably replied, 'Not all. At Lord's at the end of play men in top hats rush on to the field and hit each other with cushions!' There was not a top hat to be seen at Lord's this afternoon. Instead, one was privileged to watch two great batsmen, in two quite different styles, taking the stuffing out of first-class bowling. An infinitely superior spectacle to horseplay with cushions!

Bill Edrich, the surviving opener, is keeping Hammond stout company (Father used to worry about Edrich almost as much as Czechoslovakia as he struggled to find form against Australia in 1938), but now he's caught at slip off Australia's Ellis, not Constantine, although the latter looks, or rather expects, to take a wicket with every ball he bowls. Never again will we see a fast bowler, let alone one who's getting on a bit, race down the wicket on the completion of his delivery in the hope of plucking the ball off the bat. Then at last Hammond falls, as ever like a castle, stumped by Bremner off Cristofani for 102, his second century in the match.

England now have 6 wickets down for a score of 200. The bombarded Pavilion is beginning to cast a long shadow. But there's no question of playing for a draw. Harold Gimblett, apparently never quite as happy at Headquarters as you'll find him down at Taunton, still manages to spread a little disorder among the Dominions. Then Colonels J. G. W. Davies and S. C. Griffith carve into the bowling as if it were in the hands of a squad of raw recruits. Curiously – or significantly – enough, the records show that Keith Miller was given only 5 overs in England's blistering second innings.

Can England still win? Hopes fade when Griffith is caught at slip by the big Aussie Cedric Pepper off the leg-spin of Pettiford, but they revive when Lancashire's Phillipson seems to have no trouble in keeping up with the aggressive Davies. The trouble is that Learie Constantine never likes to be out of the picture for long. As a veteran star of the Lancashire League, he has found it incumbent upon him to steal the limelight at every possible opportunity. Now, in one movement, he picks up and throws from the depths of the country at deep mid-on, and a wicket explodes with a scampering W. E. Phillipson well short of the crease. We're down to the rabbits, Wright and Hollies, and, try as they will, they don't run, run, run. In fact, neither troubles the scorer. England are all out for 311 with 9 minutes left for play, 45 runs short of their formidable target.

No one dashes on to the field of play. We are still in the period when pitch invasions are limited to Old Harrovians with the redress of thirty-one years of failure against Eton to celebrate. Yet the cheering was as if a war was well and truly over. The players, joking and back-slapping, wend their way home to a Pavilion from which in the future, though this game may not have succeeded in setting all the post-war seasons ablaze, all manner of pleasant surprises will spring. ·

As a young National Serviceman, Duncan Kyle once bowled his medium-pacers at P. B. H. May. Born in Bradford, Kyle was a journalist until the success of his first novel, Cage of Ice, *since when he has been a full-time author.*

The Challenge

DUNCAN KYLE

No! His Lordship's negative was emphatic. However, as a fair-minded man, he *would* study the message again. He did – and said no again, for two reasons, as the saying has it. First, the challenge was not in the best interests of the game. Second, and even more important, challenge matches in general were by now part of history and ought not to be resurrected.

How and when the challenge was actually issued has become something of a mystery. The late Norman Yardley remembered Sellers and Robins cheerfully disputatious on a balcony; Kilburn has referred to mid-August; Dick Williamson, of blessed and unfailing memory, who knew most things, said the message came, as it should, from the Middlesex dressing room – the *amateur* dressing room, that is – and from the captain of Middlesex and (occasionally) of England. Full-strength sides, R. W. V. Robins insisted; neutral ground of Yorkshire's choice; and all proceeds to charity.

A. B. Sellers, he of the rolling, sailor's walk, must have bared his teeth and nodded, the way he did. He had a team, he sometimes said, which on its day could beat anyone, anywhere; furthermore, a drubbing for Master Robins would be . . . well, sweet. His wish to take up the challenge was upheld, Lord Hawke's resistance overcome – Heaven knows how, except that Arthur Sellers, Brian's father, was on the committee.

153

So to Lord's the answer sped. Yorkshire had accepted and chosen The Oval.

Now – why was all this happening? Yorkshire were champions for 1937; Middlesex runners-up. But the runners-up thought themselves the better side, and hard done by. The challenge would settle matters. Well, there has always been needle between Yorkshire and Middlesex. Not as much, perhaps, as between Middlesex and Surrey, or Yorkshire and Lancashire; but if the needle was itself a gauge smaller, it had been sharpened in that summer of 1937 by the closeness of the race. *Agamemnon* and *Cutty Sark*, tearing abreast through the Roaring Forties, is nicely analogous, considering the weather. These teams had met twice. At Lord's rain had merely interfered; at Bramall Lane, a washout.

There was much, and deep, frustration, and two fine, tough sides, with their Roman old players and their blindingly brilliant youngsters. Here were Sutcliffe and Hendren, and Compton already in an England cap at eighteen; Hutton a shade older and with ten centuries under his belt that year, one of them for England. Oh, those names! Sims, Leyland, Gubby Allen, H. G. Owen-Smith, Edrich (W. J., first and eldest of the brothers); Bowes, whom Yorkshire had once rejected and who had long ago found his way back there through application to Lord's and toil in the Nursery; Yardley and Robins, three initials apiece, printed *before* their names in the programmes of the day. Ah, yes – and an archaic word – 'truth' in Middle English, and fitting exactly the man's character, as well as his bowling – Verity. On this day, even the umpires bore great names: Chester and Hardstaff, Sen. All set. Except that on the day, Compton couldn't turn out.

Here we were, then: 11 September 1937. The challenge itself, *plus* the then significant sum of ten pounds a man; the big O of Kennington Oval with several thousand inside licking their lips.

Umpires and Beginners, please. Enter Pudsey, powerful old lion and lithe young one, Sutcliffe, H. and Hutton, L., the latter fond already of the Oval wicket and due to be much fonder within the year. It was a slow pitch that Gray bowled on and everything else was a bit slow to begin with (possible exception: Edrich, roaring acrobatically in to bowl). Sutcliffe went, eventually, for 39; Ticker Mitchell joined Hutton and the runs duly ticked, though still gently.

I was told once that Hutton's hundred and twenty-odd centuries averaged 3 hours 20 minutes each. He went on steadily for 4 hours that day, to 121, after which Yorkshire's powerful but sometimes unpredictable tail began to swing. ('Like a crocodile's, our tail,' Bowes said once.) They were still there, courtesy of a heavy shower or two, at lunch next day, by which time Mr Yardley and Mr Sellers were well on the front foot. In among all this, Jim Smith had taken three wickets in fifteen balls. What's so special? The three were Sutcliffe, Leyland and Barber, that's what. Good bowling. Big Bill Bowes, proud of taking more wickets in first-class cricket than he had scored runs, contributed his final, genial duck of the season.

Yorkshire: all out for 401.

'Rather poor light may have been a factor,' *Wisden* reports on what followed. Middlesex openers, W. F. Price (the rounded one) and G. E. Hart, were whisked away sharply, both lbw to Smailes. Then Edrich, half settled in on 13, played for Bowes's well-known third out-swinger, which swung perversely in, and was lbw also. (Was that trick picked up in the Lord's Nursery?) Now Patsy. Not *a* patsy, not by miles; this was *the* Patsy – the great Hendren, with his great engaging grin and the great record I've just looked up once more and blinked at yet again. Absorb this: 3000 runs in a season three times; 2000 twelve times; thirteen centuries in a season three times; first-class runs, 57,611. Not very tall. Quite rotund. Enormously liked and admired. And today playing his absolutely final match for Middlesex. Hear the greeting they give him!

Bad light by now and a slow pitch, and the tall Bowes surprisingly quick and bouncy on it; but down goes Patsy's grizzled chin and he grafts purposefully. Run here, run there, but perhaps the superb old reflexes a mite slower now, and the eye on this dank day not so instant. Pity his farewell is not in sunshine and at Lord's, where his happy heart resides. He's on 17 when Bowes does for him. Round the ground, tears well up as Patsy goes – from middle-aged men who'd watched him for thirty years, and from boys who would never now see his wonders.

Robins, instigator of the whole thing, next got a single and went. Not very exciting, just now. Depressing, even. But. . . . In strides the modest, neat, compact, formidable South African, Owen-Smith, double Blue, international full back; forearms like Popeye and the eye of a falcon. Batting now, first with Felton, then Jim Sims and Smith, both also powerful, he simply hit. Yorkshire dropped catches the way

sides do when a hitter has an on day. Owen-Smith drove and drove again at Verity, made 77, and the last four Middlesex wickets put on 121. The lethal Verity had a mere 2 for 51, which by the standards of *his* analyses on wet wickets, was almost failure. Still, despite those brave final stands Middlesex followed on. And now the pitch was drying rapidly, almost steaming as it turned violent.

Really, there's not much to say beyond that. Price was hurt, in opening, and Verity then marched off briskly with all the wickets left (except for Owen-Smith's). Eight for 43 in 12½ overs. Yorkshire won by an innings and plenty.

As a match it's remembered, if at all, as an ultimately disappointing curiosity. But it produced several things I'd give a bit to see next season: a clean hundred from the young Hutton; the farewell to one of the very greatest; and powerful, attacking amateurs of spirit, one of whom smacked round the ground one of the finest of all spinners.

It also generated a little rhyme I learned at school that autumn:

> Who killed Cock Robins?
> I, said Brian Sellers,
> With my noble band of fellers.
> I killed Cock Robins.

(But would it have been the same if the match had been played whence the challenge came? At Lord's? Ed.)

Just as comparatively few writers concentrated on a particular match, so relatively few zoned in on a particular physical part of Lord's. The three following pieces are exceptions. Michael Green has written twenty-three books and plays but is probably best known for his series entitled The Art of Coarse. . . . *His two volumes of autobiography,* The Boy Who Shot Down an Airship *and* Nobody Hurt in Small Earthquake, *are not only full of cricket, they're also very funny. Here he recalls the old Tavern.*

The Tavern

MICHAEL GREEN

It came as something of a shock when I realized the other day that not many people under forty will remember the old Tavern at Lord's, now demolished for more than twenty years. When I first came to London in the early 1950s as a sub-editor on the long-lost evening newspaper *The Star*, it was the Mecca of all true cricket-lovers, pointed out to foreigners as an example of typical Englishness in sport, and something that would last, like all English traditions, for ever. Unfortunately, the MCC thought otherwise and pulled it down.

When I say 'the Tavern' I don't mean the pub itself. This was a huge, stark, Victorian gin-palace which faced two ways. There was an entrance in the road outside and that section was an ordinary pub. Then there was another section at the back which opened on to the cricket ground, with no connection between the two except the central bar serving area. To cricket-lovers, the Tavern meant not only the back bar but the standing space outside it which bordered the boundary.

Despite the fact that the view was awful with a full house, as the area wasn't properly terraced, here used to gather a unique collection of cricket fans, knowledgeable, bibulous and, above all, talkative. Most of them arrived after work, about the time of the tea interval, although that beverage was rarely drunk. A great many came from the stage or what we now call the media and at about six o'clock there might be a sudden stirring as some of the actors left for their West End theatres. Foremost among them was Spike Hughes, author of *The Art of Coarse Cricket*, a book which could be said to have been born upon the terrace outside the Tavern as he yarned with his friends.

Spike was a legendary figure, a former Fleet Street columnist, a notable jazz musician, the world's greatest living authority on Mozart, and author of a definitive world dictionary of opera. He was also cricket-mad and his book for the first time did justice to those heroes of the game who keep it alive with nine men and a dog on a Sunday afternoon in some remote pasture. *Coarse Cricket* was, in fact, the first of the long series of *Coarse* sporting books. My own, *The Art of Coarse Rugby*, followed on from Spike, with his blessing.

Spike was a founder-member of the Lord's Taverners, then just an occasional informal drinking group of people who met in front of the Tavern. He bitterly resented its expansion into a respectable and famous charity-supporting organization and in fact resigned when the Duke of Edinburgh was appointed Twelfth Man, because he felt the whole thing had become too formal. Fortunately, he was persuaded to return.

Sometimes down there I would meet John Slater, then famous as the veteran Sergt Stone of 'Z Cars'. I played cricket against him once, when he used to turn out for the Stage CC. The match was at Eton and John was due in the West End to appear in a play at 7.30. Coming in at six o'clock, he hit out desperately in an effort to score quickly and then get out, with the result that he made 64 in less than half an hour before I caught him on the boundary. He had a chauffeur-driven car waiting for him by the changing-room and was running towards it while the ball was still in the air. Obviously he had more faith in my fielding than the skipper had.

Lots of BBC people were Tavern regulars, among them an old friend from my Birmingham days, Reggie Smith, a senior radio drama producer. Reggie's chief claim to fame, though, was that he was married to the novelist Olivia Manning, author of *The Balkan Trilogy*, which was such a success when the BBC televized it in 1988. Reggie was the original Guy, the husband of Harriet Pringle, the heroine, and boasted gently of the fact. He didn't seem bothered by his wife's portrayal of him as an eccentric, rather neglectful husband, more interested in his theatre activities than his marriage; indeed, he was immensely proud of her reputation and the success of her books, a success largely due to her masterly portrait of himself. Reggie, a great shambling bear of a man, brought some tone to the proceedings, as befitted a drama producer, especially when lubricated with the beer he drank in large quantities. I shall never forget him chastising a Middlesex player who dropped a catch right in front of us on the boundary with the words, 'Compared with you, old chap, Oedipus Rex was eagle-eyed', an allusion which brought knowing laughter from the Tavern regulars, although it was perhaps lost on the large Australian contingent who gathered there, one of whom bellowed, 'Who does this joker Oedipus play for, then?' But the Tavern was the home of barracking. When a wicket fell or a chance was missed, people in other parts of the ground used to look over there in anticipation of some witticism and they weren't often disappointed.

Another of the theatrical crowd who sometimes met at the Tavern was Basil Thomas. Basil's family deserves a niche in the history of both the stage and cricket as founders of a famous Midland theatrical cricketing side, The Reptiles. This was based on actors and staff of the Grand Theatre, Wolverhampton, where Basil was manager, and the Alexandra Theatre, Birmingham, owned by his cousin Derek Salberg. Derek was a theatrical impresario in the great tradition of Frank Benson, the Victorian actor–manager, who is alleged to have sent a telegram from Stratford-on-Avon saying, 'Send fast bowler to play Laertes immediately.' The Reptiles not only played every week in Birmingham but went on tour to Buckinghamshire every year, where they recruited extra men like Reggie Smith and myself. Another of their fans was John Laurie, later to become the undertaker in 'Dad's Army', although he never played. But he remained a supporter and a Tavern man.

Basil was not very good at cricket so he compensated by becoming the team statistician and humorist. In Volume Two of my autobiography, *Nobody Hurt in Small Earthquake*, I've described how, when we played Gerrard's Cross on tour, they included a lot of young public schoolboys who wrote their best scores on the backs of their bats, thus: 'Eighty-six *v* Repton; fifty-three *v* Harrow'. When Basil came to the wicket for his usual brief stay he retaliated by writing on the back of his own bat: 'Nought v Woolworth's; five v Marks and Spencer's'. This puzzled the young opponents considerably and I could see them trying to work it out as they crouched down behind the wicket or in the slips. Later Basil wrote a successful West End farce, *Book of the Month*, and on the strength of it abandoned the Grand Theatre to come to London as a full-time writer, being the author of a film starring Arthur Askey.

Not everybody outside the Tavern was from the stage or media, of course. It's just that they happened to form a closely knit nucleus which tended to set the tone of the proceedings. The crowd was the usual mixed bunch, from office workers (who found it a very popular spot, despite the constant danger of meeting their bosses) to booze-artists. One such was suddenly sick near Reggie Smith's feet and he swiftly retaliated by gently remarking, 'Ah, that's better out than in.' Not that such behaviour was common. Lord's was a pretty strict place in the 1950s and gentlemen were requested to wear shirts. Offenders bare to the waist were escorted from the ground by attendants.

That wouldn't happen today, of course, and perhaps it's better not to be too nostalgic about the old Tavern and to realize times have changed. After all, it was an era when professional cricketers playing in front of the Tavern were distinguished from amateurs by having their initials put after their names, while amateurs followed the normal practice (F. R. Brown but Hutton, L.). That seems as incredible today as dear old Basil writing 'Nought v Woolworth's' on the back of his bat or someone being thrown out for not wearing a shirt. Perhaps it's just as well the Tavern was pulled down while we have largely happy memories of it and the cheerful gang who gathered there.

Michael Marshall, the Conservative MP for Arundel since 1974 (how could he not be a cricket enthusiast when representing that constituency?) has written books on Jack Buchanan, Stanley Holloway, dramatic monologues and Gentlemen and Players. He takes us to the top of the Pavilion.

On Top of the World

MICHAEL MARSHALL

The distinguished stranger sitting next to me on the top tier of the Pavilion at Lord's asked if I knew the name of the Sikh fielder below us. When I replied, 'Bishan Bedi' and, showing off, added the rest of the Indian fielding side, he asked about my interest in the game. On discovering that this was based on past cricket commentating activities rather than increasingly unremarkable performances for the Lords and Commons XI or at the Arundel Castle Cricket Club, we moved on to cricketing authors.

By a lengthy process which need not detain the reader, it was established that, while my cricket writing interest was simmering, a first book with a theatrical theme was on the boil. It was further established that the subject concerned, the late Jack Buchanan, was the object of both the interrogator's as well as the writer's warm regard.

The day went pleasantly by with the England batsmen, in those near but seemingly far-off days, showing their ability to compile a huge total against spin-bowling, and with shared theatrical and sporting memories between overs. During the tea interval our paths diverged and it was with real regret that, on returning to my seat, I found the distinguished stranger had gone.

A few days later, a letter arrived at the House of Commons saying, in effect, that if I were still looking for a publisher, 'we would be delighted

to take on the job'. It was signed Jaimie Hamish Hamilton. For those, like me, who have struggled to get a long-established publisher, such as Hamish Hamilton, for their first book, the significance of this offer will not be lost. Nearer to our theme, however, it was my first recognition of the unique nature of the audience attracted to the top tier of the Pavilion at Lord's.

In the years which have followed, I have come to recognize that the late Jaimie Hamish Hamilton was far from alone in representing the literary world at Lord's. Climb the three flights of stairs from the back door of the Pavilion during a Test match and there sits Pavilion Books; there is André Deutsch and Collins Willow. Despite the claims of the press box in faraway Warner land, representatives from *The Cricketer* and *Wisden's Cricket Monthly* show their preference for the Eagle's Nest, and *The Cricket Society Journal* holds court to a flock of statisticians.

From these early literary discoveries has come a recognition of the many others with a passion for cricket on high. Some, such as the authors or the actors, are a logical extension of the publishers, but they bring a certain glamour to the proceedings. For they include the star names – those sporting the salmon and cucumber colours of the Garrick or the red, blue and green of the Lord's Taverners – who can have their pick of invitations to the Committee and other boxes and yet prefer the serious business of watching cricket from an ideal vantage point. I recall the happy hours spent listening to the late Ben Travers and his first-hand impressions of W.G.; to the cricket world and theatre of (good) manners of Michael Denison; and to the no less courteous but more contemporary views on the modern game of Michael Jayston.

But these literary and theatrical figures are not alone in providing entertainment off the field. The very structure of the top tier might have been designed for the purpose. With its entrances at either wing and in the centre, there is a constant ebb and flow. And the gangways, both vertical and horizontal in the outdoor and undercover sections, all encourage the formation of groupings with their distinctive colours.

Here sit the Middlesex supporters, there Surrey, and there Essex, bringing their shared scimitars and Prince of Wales' feathers and a welcome touch of irreverence in what might otherwise be a rarified atmosphere. Close proximity and joint membership explain their presence, but what brings the Wombwell Cricket Lovers Society all the way from Yorkshire in such numbers and on such regular occasions? With the foot soldiers from such clubs comes a variety of colour to contrast with the regular army of MCC members in their standard issue of orange and gold. The mixture is further heightened by the old school tie brigade, whose Ramblers, Waifs, Friars, Wanderers, Rangers and Pilgrims have seemingly found at least one common meeting ground.

Among them one may glimpse the schoolboy heroes – not in the Dexter, May or Cowdrey class, called to higher things in the TCCB or President's Box – but here are the cricket masters who, with their professional partners, helped to steer them on their way. These are the heirs to the Rockley Wilson and 'Father' Marriott school of coaching – not, in these professional days, able to move as they did in and out of county and even Test cricket, but good enough to lead by example and to find satisfaction in contributing to each new generation of cricketers.

Gathered around them one may see some of the results. Some have added to the romance of the game as the 'nearly men': the wartime Oxbridge captain for whom military service and a medical career meant the end of serious cricket ambitions; the soccer Blue who was twelfth man for Oxford at Lord's in successive years and who, just to show his versatility, won the All India Rugby tournament for Madras with place kicking of obscene length; and, perhaps most maddeningly of all for lesser mortals, the schoolboy genius who took 70 off one of the MCC's best pace attacks before, typically, giving away his wicket while late cutting off the middle stump and retiring permanently from the game.

The same evidence of former youthful exuberance can be found in the serious occupations represented on the top tier. One of the most regular attenders is a churchman whose identity remains unknown to the author but whose conversation brings to mind the long tradition of first-class cricketing clerics and whose beatific smile is reminiscent of the late Bishop of Bath and Wells who, it was said, occupied his mind during the long walk up the nave of his cathedral with a serious contemplation of the prospects of getting the ball to turn if he pitched his leg-spinner on the rough patch just in front of the altar.

Similarly, the lawyers and the businessmen, whose dark suits indicate their early morning office attendance (but whose 'consultations with clients' have since taken on a distinctly light-hearted air), give every impression of a well-spent youth. There is one company chairman, a former golfing Blue and serious drinking member of his college cricket team (for whom I happened to be working at the time and whose permission had not been sought in taking time off from the office), who showed his quality by saying, 'I won't tell if you don't.' One thinks, too, of the judge who followed his father into the first-class game and whose court sittings conveniently end in time for him to join his friends in that elevated part of the Pavilion to which his father introduced him.

Then there are the retired. They can be observed on the morning of any international match in large numbers outside the Grace Gates. When the gates open at nine o'clock they demonstrate a turn of speed belying their years in climbing rapidly to the top of the Pavilion and establishing their favoured vantage points. Nor should their retirement be regarded as a passive occupation. One recognizes many who serve on county committees. Their doyen is a former impresario who has performed wonders for the marketing of both Surrey County Cricket Club and the TCCB. Bernie Coleman is typical of those who refuse grand invitations for entertainment elsewhere to indulge in the serious business of cricket watching from behind the bowler's arm. He brings to the Lord's community an international flavour, too. True to his principles, on his regular winter travels he can be found on top of the pavilion in Sydney, Antigua, Bombay, Lahore or Wellington. He is thus a natural focal point for MCC's overseas visitors, with a supporting cast which ranges from Indian princes to Australian I Zingari and players from around the world.

What are the attractions that bring this international gathering as well as the British regulars to this particular part of the Pavilion at Lord's? The ground floor has its adherents with a sense of closeness to the players and the opportunity of sharing the dignity of the Long Room or the quiet of the reading room. Of the cramped middle floor balcony the best that can be said is that it may be useful for compulsive gamblers for whom proximity to the telephone is the first priority.

By contrast, the top tier is a self-contained world of its own. It provides the best vantage point for the whole of the ground as well as wicket to wicket. It has a convivial bar, from whose balcony, which is relatively uncrowded by comparison with the scrum on the ground floor, it is even possible to watch the game. The members' dining room enjoys a similar advantage, while offering better seafood than that found elsewhere on the ground. Dining there gives a sense of shared occasion with the players as they tuck into their roast and several vegetables in the adjoining room. Those who have had the good fortune to be invited to join them can readily understand why it is regarded as a culinary high spot on the cricketing tour.

But it is in the assembled company – the gallery that looks down on cricket's greatest stage – that the top of the Pavilion creates its unique atmosphere. They also have the special advantage of their messengers to the world. For surely 'Test Match Special' has a rightful claim as the brightest jewel in the gothic crown of Lord's, and its participants do much to set the tone of proceedings off the field. Their entrances and exits are as closely observed as those of the players. Nowadays the state visits of Jim Swanton, with the elegant Band of Brothers Panama hat, are a rare event, but treasured all the more by those with a taste for cricket's own form of papal blessing. His place as the senior BBC pro has been taken by Brian Johnston. His comings and goings in co-respondent shoes with booming bonhomie bring a smile like a tidal wave across the faces in the crowd. So, too, does the 'My dear old thing' cry of 'Blowers', Henry Blofeld, dressed as often as not in a safari jacket reminiscent of the days when it was said that he was reporting for three quarters of the world's cricket press. Trevor Bailey greets the Essex faithful on arrival and times his departures with precision in responding to luncheon invitations. Christopher Martin-Jenkins brings a studious air to the task of sending the Lord's message in both written and spoken form to the world.

Apart from the parade of their regulars, much of the interest in the 'Test Match Special' presence relates to its Command Performances. These are the special invitations sent to distinguished cricket-lovers during each Lord's Test match for an interview during the lunch interval. In the 1980s Ben Travers, Brian Rix, Michael Bentine, Peter Tinniswood (and his brigadier, Robin Bailey), Bernard Cribbins, Christopher Lee, Robert Powell and David Essex have all brought show business to the commentary box, while serious music was represented by Julian Bream in 1986, with the royal accolade in 1987 when the guest of honour was the Duke of Edinburgh.

Is it any wonder that those who favour the top tier do so because of its guaranteed entertainment value? Indeed, in this self-contained world rain can sometimes come as a blessed relief – depending on the cricket – in allowing opportunities to recall past England triumphs or the joys of cricket up and down the land. Of course, it is élitist, but so is the MCC and it can surely be argued that this peer group is widely drawn. The only danger in writing of the top tier is that it may increase the competition for places in the early morning scramble. Still, true to the author's political colours, how can one deny the virtues of such competition and the rich prizes waiting for those willing to climb the stairs?

Tony Winlaw, stalwart match manager and occasional captain of I Zingari, is a National Hunt handicapper out of season but can usually be found reporting county cricket somewhere or other for someone or other. Once upon a time he was Swanton's 'gofer' at The Daily Telegraph. Here he leads us across the bridge to 'Q'.

The Question of 'Q'

A. S. R. de W. WINLAW

I had been an MCC member for more than twenty-one years before I discovered the joys of Upper Q Stand. Now one looks back and tries to fathom how and why a member could possibly have missed such a Club feature.

Because MCC is a club, however, no advertisement, direction or sign is required to encourage further persons to join the Q Stand regulars. The Upper Stand is only open on major match days and you can only get in by appearing to enter none other than the England dressing room! There, at the closed door, sits a rather forbidding-looking attendant. After a nervous turn of the handle, you are still not quite into the hallowed quarters. There is a narrow passageway and then, after turning sharp right, you go over a romantic bridge (no ladies – just Incogs, Arabs, Cryptics, Foresters, etc.) and into the comfort of 'Q'.

The lower deck of the stand is open for players and their families, and Middlesex members, but above only club members are allowed. There is invariably a spare seat among the familiar figures present for every Test match.

At the back of the stand there is the friendliest of bars. This is run by two genial and long-suffering ladies, Jean and Rita, who, until recently, were in charge of the famous Cottage Rake bar at Cheltenham racecourse. It is certainly a privilege to savour a glass of Pimm's and enjoy the panoramic view of the field of play, without a push or disturbance all day.

Here are many former players and 'Giants of Old', fancy and meaningful neckwear to the fore. John Edrich and John Price are two regulars and, when not engaged in the proceedings, David Gower is a figurehead. There are plenty of Hampshire Hogs on parade and the 'Q' bar is a popular sanctum for Hampshire captains Ingleby-Mackenzie, Pocock and Nicholas. Sir William Becher usually arrives for drinks at mid-day, doubtless to discuss important I Zingari matters with Colonel Havergal and Peter Delisle (Oxford and Middlesex). Peter Lowndes is often seen with many a fellow Eton Rambler; Nick Craig, all the way from Northumberland, never misses a ball; Richard Hutton may also be there, probably with his Yorkshire and England colleague Don Wilson; Wray Eller, in Gemini tie, takes his annual back-row seat by the bar; and, not to be missed, also to be found there is that sports writers' agent, John Dorman, who, quite correctly, once reminded me that 'business is never to be discussed in Upper Q Stand'.

Whereas these are some of the regulars, there are others, in fact, who claim to be almost 'partners' of Q Stand. They are a select number – less than twenty persons – who have formed a club-within-a-club. Membership, by invitation only, is secretive enough, almost masonic – as far as inquisitive persons such as myself are concerned, although I am assured that the Australian High Commissioner in London is a member. The qualification for membership appears to be 'the ability to enjoy good company, lively conversation and generosity for several glasses of one's favourite tipple throughout the day'. The 'club' has its own tie and, like MCC, there is a country and a city version. The country tie consists of a crossed bottle, bat and the letter 'Q' in red on a yellow background, whilst the city tie has the same motif in pink on a dark blue background.

I'm afraid the qualification of 'lively conversation' has ruined my personal hopes of membership. If rain stops play, or England are defending, or anyone will listen, I invariably tell my story of Len Hutton and the bowler whom he 'feared', Ken Farnes. And Editor or no Editor I am going to tell it here. After all, it *does* concern Lord's as well as my hero Hutton.

I was first introduced to Sir Leonard Hutton at the Headingley Test match, when I was E. W. Swanton's secretary, in 1959. The great

England captain made his first-class debut against Cambridge in 1934, when he was run out, by J. G. W. Davies from cover point, for 0. My father, R. de W. K. Winlaw, was playing for the university and, in fact, scored a hundred before Yorkshire won by ten wickets. Sir Leonard remembered the name and was very kind to me that day at Headingley. He even invited me to the President's Box, where the *Yorkshire Evening Post* took a photograph of us watching play. Any conceit, however, vanished when this appeared on the front page under the heading: 'Sir Len and son Richard at the Test'!

I'm sorry, I will get to Lord's in a minute. . . .

During that Test match I plucked up courage and stupidly asked Sir Len, 'Who were the fastest bowlers you ever faced?' He quickly replied, 'I have seen lots of fast bowlers – son.' A long silence followed, but just before I turned too scarlet in the face, he added, 'There are only two bowlers whom I *feared*.' Another silence followed before he revealed their names: 'Ken Farnes, who played for Cambridge with your father, and Keith Miller, who is over there in the press box.'

It was in the Gentlemen *v* Players match at Lord's in 1938 that Farnes was such a fearsome figure, 'never to be forgotten', said Hutton. This tall (6 ft 5 in) Essex fast bowler – a master at Worksop College later killed while flying on active service in 1941 – had just been dropped from the England team for the Third Test match against the Australians at Old Trafford. In fact, not a ball was bowled because of rain. The match following was Gentlemen *v* Players.

Farnes was reputedly a most good-natured fast bowler, but his omission from the England Test team had clearly aroused his anger. Few had observed such temperament from Farnes but the future England captain was well aware of it. The Gentlemen scored 411 (H. T. Bartlett, 175 not out; N. W. D. Yardley, 88) on the opening day to leave the Players little more than 10 minutes' batting. It was in this time that the fear of Farnes arose, as he dismissed both Bill Edrich and Fred Price for 0 in the same over. Farnes finished with 8 for 43, regained his place in the England team, and the Gentlemen beat the Players at Lord's for only the second time since the First World War.

In 1980, when the Gillette company, after eighteen years, gave up sponsorship of the first-ever limited-over competition in this country, that fine cricket impresario the late Gordon Ross kindly invited me to their farewell dinner. I was on table 50-odd but, at port and wash-time,

I suddenly saw Len Hutton sitting 'spare' at the top table. I could not resist approaching him before the speeches. It was twenty-one years since I had asked – or rather, was told – of that fearsome Farnes. So, with all that Gillette smoothness behind me, I enquired once more, 'Were there any bowlers you ever feared?' A long delay – not quite the red-faced length of Headingley – but this time his response was, 'What an interesting question. I will have to think.' After a bet or two in my head, his answer was still that same 1959 pair, Farnes and Miller.

The top table filled and the interest increased as Sir Len recalled Farnes's fury and pace in that Gentlemen and Players match, but then his new table companion interrupted and exclaimed, 'I don't think that you ever faced him that evening, Len – you were much too clever for that.' It was Bill Edrich and he reminded Len that 'as we went through the tunnel [professionals did not then come down the Pavilion steps] you said to me, "Let's go as we are." I agreed, not, anyway, being a specialist opener. Then, when we surfaced on to the field of play, you repeated, "Yes – let's go as we are!"' That meant Edrich facing Farnes. Edrich recalled: 'I never saw the first ball; the second hit me in the face and I collapsed "dead". When I eventually rose to face the next delivery those so-called Gentlemen appealed and I was given out – caught off the handle, via the face, and into the hands of an Army officer [J. W. A. Stephenson] in the gully.'

Hutton might have turned a shade of Headingley red, but then Edrich added that Farnes had 'cooled off next morning and you went on to make top score, Len [52]'.

The following season (1981) I was reporting a match at Fenner's for *The Daily Telegraph* when I spotted N. W. D. Yardley gazing at the engraved Cambridge XIs on the boards. When he reached those Farnes years of 1931–3 I interrupted to recount the Edrich tale. Norman Yardley duly confirmed the high speed of Farnes and added that there was more to the story! He said that Joe Hardstaff (Nottinghamshire), after watching the first ball, was definitely 'unfit to bat'. Frank Woolley, who in his last year, aged fifty-one, was accorded the honour of captaining the Players, sent in the night-watchman Fred Price, the Middlesex wicket-keeper. Yardley remembered Price retreating from the fastest of all deliveries only to be effortlessly caught in the slips by the Gentlemen's captain Wally Hammond.

Later in the season I was reporting Leicestershire *v* Scotland, in the Benson and Hedges Cup, at Grace Road. The adjudicator was none other than Joe Hardstaff and, of course, I had to ask about the speed of Farnes! Hardstaff duly confirmed it: 'I will never forget it. . . . After seeing the first Farnes flyer, I exclaimed to Fred Price, "I don't fancy that much." Price proudly retorted, "Those Gents wouldn't scare me – you wet – I'll go in next." I jumped at the offer and retired to the loo, as Frank Woolley was told that I wasn't feeling too well. I certainly was not!' He continued, saying that, towards the end of his distinguished career (1930–55), 'I was batting quite well at Trent Bridge and had scored about 70 runs when the opponents – Somerset, I think – introduced an amateur "occasional bowler" to deliver the last over of the day. The first ball, well flighted, went down the leg side and grazed the outside of my pad. The gentleman mumbled half an appeal but, surprisingly, I was given out lbw. In those days we walked forthwith and that was that. But in the evening – I admit that I had enjoyed a glass or two – I couldn't stop myself from saying to the umpire, "That was a nasty thing you did to me out there." He replied, "It was a nasty thing you did to me in 1938."' The umpire was, of course, Fred Price.

This might not be sufficiently 'lively conversation' to qualify for Q Stand membership, but surely it confirms the pace of Farnes and the wisdom of Hutton?

Hugh Montgomery-Massingberd, the Daily Telegraph's *obituary editor, resident genealogist, historic-house expert, and all-round feature writer, has to come in immediately after Winlaw because he is his half-brother. It was Winlaw who occasioned Massingberd's first visit to Lord's. Montgomery-Massingberd is the only man I know who can carry off an I Zingari striped blazer and flannels on a train journey to Shrewsbury.*

Talking of Winlaw

HUGH MONTGOMERY-MASSINGBERD

Arriving at Lord's Cricket Ground, even on a wet weekday morning in the close season, I felt strangely excited, awe-struck and apprehensive. Perhaps because I'm pretty hopeless at it, the great game has always induced mixed emotions, dominated by a desperate sort of stage fright (cricket and the theatre having strong links).

The deep-seated horror of, say, dropping a catch doubtless goes back to early childhood when I was obliged to field in highly competitive family Tests on the lawn organized by my elder half-brother, A. S. R. de W. Winlaw (later to be a cricket reporter). I remember rushing blubbing from the field after failing to hold on to a skyer and then sulking in the woodshed, where I would alternately curse cricket and Winlaw to extinction or fantasize about scoring hundreds at Lord's.

My first visit to Lord's was in 1955 to see Winlaw play in the Eton *v* Harrow match – the ground's oldest fixture, which happened to be celebrating its 150th anniversary.

Lord Byron appeared in 1805 in the first match played at Thomas Lord's ground, then in Dorset Square; on account of his club foot, the poet batted with a runner and scored 7 and 2 – at least, according to the scorebook kept at Lord's. The scorers could, however, have been confused by the presence of a runner and may have awarded several of Byron's notches to his batting partner, Shakespeare (nobody can say cricket is not a literary game).

When I walked through the Grace Gates – or, more likely, pushed through the turnstiles – 150 years on, the Eton and Harrow was still a considerable social occasion. There were carriages parked round the boundaries and the scene was reminiscent of that depicted in A. Chevallier Taylor's charming little oil of 1886 in the Long Room. The present Pavilion was actually built four years after Taylor's painting, but in 1955 I seem to remember my grandmother sitting under a similar tented awning where the unsympathetic Warner Stand was to be erected a few years later.

In the luncheon interval there was a fashionable promenade on the sacred Lord's turf. The fantastic apparition of Barbara Cartland, with her daughter Raine (then Mrs Gerald Legge) in tow, hove into view. I had recently been learning about the French Revolution and as I crept about the ground in my short grey trousers I began to understand the sentiments of the sans-culottes.

The experience was so overwhelming that I declined to return the following day (missing, I was assured, a close finish). Instead, I settled down in the woodshed to write the first of many cricketing novels featuring the dashing exploits of my alter ego, styled – I blush to recall – 'Sir Julian Jeremy Bruce, Bt, MA, OBE, VC'. I would fill exercise book after exercise book with the most detailed descriptions and scores of imaginary matches played by fictional characters, all written up in a style that leant more heavily, I fear, on the ghosted memoirs of contemporary players than on the prose of the *Daily Telegraph*'s great E. W. Swanton. Then, having checked that the coast was clear, I would swagger out on to my secret pitch and act out the fantasy, frequently holding my bat aloft and doffing one of Winlaw's caps to the cheers of the non-existent crowd.

The reality was rather different, and in the hope of improving my cricketing ability I was sent up to Lord's for one of MCC's coaching courses in the Easter holidays. The distinctive carbolic and jockstrap smell of the changing-rooms floated back to me down the stairs when I returned to the Pavilion recently to write a piece about the ground's treasures.

All I can remember of the coaching was feeling utterly inadequate while surly old pros stood around looking understandably fed up. Once we spotted the sleek figures of Ronny Aird and Billy Griffith, the Secretary and Assistant Secretary respectively of Marylebone Cricket Club; and one wet afternoon the curator of Lord's, Miss Diana Rait Kerr, lectured us on the history of cricket. The only point that stuck in my mind was that 'cricket' was a diminutive of *cric*, Anglo-Saxon for a curved staff or crook.

I'm sorry to say that this intimate exposure to Lord's at an early age did not instil in me a particular affection for the place. Although, to my amazement, I was picked for the Harrow Colts against Eton, I later languished on the fringes of the Third XI and there was not the remotest possibility that I might ever play at Lord's.

For several years I went through the motions of playing for various wandering clubs into which Winlaw had kindly shoe-horned me, although most of the time I was either in a state of complete funk or wondering what on earth I was doing there. A rare highlight was capturing the scalp of the Star of India, the Nawab of Pataudi (ct. Winlaw, b. Massingberd 144), on a village pitch in Hampshire.

There was talk of my being put up for membership of MCC, but somehow it never happened. I came to regard Lord's from a distance as stuffy, self-satisfied and smug. Finding myself living in Kennington, I regularly whiled away the long freelance afternoons at The Oval, which struck me as engagingly down-to-earth and friendly. I realized how much I liked the old gasometer ground when I happened to be sitting behind two MCC members who had migrated south of the river for one last Test. One of them unwisely stood up at a critical moment. 'Siddown!' snarled a Surrey stalwart to my left. 'You can tell we're at The Oval,' said the injured party, and his companion underlined the point by indicating the sign on the pavilion fence bearing the legend: 'Members Are Requested To Keep Their Shirts On At All Times'. 'Wouldn't see that at Lord's, what?' he sniffed.

It was at The Oval, after all, I reminded myself as I waited to be shown round the Lord's Pavilion, that the very first England *v* Australia Test match was played, *not* at Lord's. And yet where did they play the centenary game in 1980? Yes, you've guessed it: Lord's. No amount of South London bravado, however, could disguise the fact that I was at Headquarters and feeling nervous.

Among the pictures I was shown on my tour, I particularly liked the portrait of the scorer (a jovial old josser fortified by an enormous bottle) and the sketch of C. Aubrey Smith (Charterhouse, Cambridge, Sussex, MCC, England and Hollywood). I recalled the story of how the old actor, then very deaf, assumed from the animated nature of the conversation around him at a Hollywood dinner party that the merits of some sport were being argued – although, in fact, the subject under discussion was homosexuality. Smith spoke up: 'Well, whatever you say, give me three stumps, a bat and a ball.'

In the Memorial Gallery behind the Pavilion I am diverted by some of the more curious relics of the game, such as the nulla-nulla used by the Aborigine Dick-a-Dick on the 1868 tour of England, the emu's egg trophy, and the stuffed sparrow mounted on the ball that killed it at Lord's in 1936 ('both ball and bird were declared dead'). I recalled that I had met the bowler concerned, the late Jahangir Khan, who gave me lunch at Veeraswamy's as a boy – no Indian meal has ever seemed quite the same since. The great Khan was a team-mate of my mother's first husband, R. de W. K. Winlaw (Winchester, Cambridge, Surrey and Bedfordshire).

Then, suddenly, there were the Ashes themselves – surprisingly small, like the Bayeux Tapestry. 'Good Lord,' I said, noticing an insignificant plaque at the bottom of the display case. There, for the first time, I read that the case had been presented in memory of Roger Winlaw and his fellow cricketer, Claud Ashton, who were killed together while serving with the RAF in 1942.

Suddenly I felt at home. Who knows, perhaps one day I might even belong?

Publisher, television executive, and sometime England wing-three-quarter, Derek Wyatt is an intriguing contrast to the traditionalism of Winlaw and Montgomery-Massingberd. Not orthodox.

Ghostly Reflections

DEREK WYATT

Middlesex were playing Surrey. Peter May, the darling of the Establishment, was batting. He was the reality. Roy of the Rovers was his comic equivalent. I knew him better. Rain set in. Lunch was taken early for the second time that morning as we'd scoffed ours within minutes of boarding a bus from Mill Hill. It continued to rain, so we decided to go to the flicks to see *The Sinking of the Titanic*.

My mother became twitchy at around three o'clock. She'd heard on the wireless that play had been abandoned for the day and so was expecting me home. By 4.00 p.m. she was apoplectic and when I finally arrived home, soaked, at six, she was not amused. In due course, my father gave me my customary beating of the week. Subsequent visits to Lord's did not feature high on my hit list.

It was twenty-six years before I ventured there again. I'd frequently sneaked out of school to watch Essex CCC, especially when another youngster, K. W. R. Fletcher, was playing, but Twickenham and Wimbledon beckoned more frequently.

In 1984 we'd just had our first experience of a blackwash from the West Indies. A *Private Eye* cartoon captured it brilliantly – it showed a coach parked outside the Grace Gates emblazoned with the initials MCC, with the destination on the back of the window marked 'To Lourdes'. I was back at Lord's by invitation. Allan Lamb, England's hero of the West Indian series, had suggested we meet during the less frenetic Test against Sri Lanka. He'd supplied two tickets so I was able to invite my father as well. Funny, I kept wanting to go to a movie. I needed to talk to Allan because we had signed him to write his autobiography. Well, that's not quite true. We'd signed Allan Lamb to talk to Peter Smith, then the cricket correspondent of the *Daily Mail* and head ghostwriter, to do his 'autobiography'. *Lamb's Tales* was duly published in 1985 with an Adrian Murrell picture of Ian Botham holding a piece of paper over Lamb's mouth. Though it was a ghosted book I had decided to put Peter Smith's name on the cover. I hadn't originally commissioned the book and I wanted to draw attention to the part a 'ghost' plays. It still annoys me that writers such as Angela Patmore, who was responsible for Mike Gatting's *Leading from the Front*, aren't credited on the cover.

Lord's has become a regular home for me since I moved from teaching via Oxford and journalism to publishing and television. Cricket literature is strong and vibrant (though the same cannot be said for cricket book sales, despite the large numbers of books published each year).

In 1985 I published Gerald Pawle's *R. E. S. Wyatt*. Bob Wyatt came up from his Cornish home to the launch party at Lord's and took in the Second Test against the Australians, which they duly won by four wickets with Allan Border scoring 196 in the first innings and 41 not out in the second. It was their only win in the series. Bob sat next to Gubby Allen and was reported to have said to him, 'Gather you're the bastard son of Plum Warner.' This rumour bounced off the back of the Long Room before he'd finished the sentence. I'd heard it several times before and had been disappointed that in E. W. Swanton's study *Gubby Allen: Man of Cricket*, also published that year, all he'd stated was, 'Gubby was born on 31 July 1902 in the house built by his father in Victoria Road, Bellevue Hill, only a ten-minute drive from the heart of Sydney.' Fortunately, I had commissioned Gerald Howat to write the biography of Sir Pelham Warner (1987) so he was charged with settling this once and for all. Gerald tried to track down whether Plum had met Mrs Marguerite Allen in October 1901 but, alas, to no avail. Yet, the rumour persists. Of course, 1985 also saw the Australian-produced television series on 'Bodyline' which captured our imagination. Cricket purists hated it. In a sense it was a shame the BBC hadn't done its own version. Indeed, David Puttnam, following the success of

Chariots of Fire, had looked at 'Bodyline' as a possible successor, but, apparently, legal complications set in and it was dropped. Pity.

Being a publisher has drawn me into the notion that there is some sort of cricket conspiracy that emanates from Lord's. I was first made aware of this by the greatest living Zambian cricketer, Phil Edmonds. Edmonds, like Lamb, doesn't suffer fools gladly. Yet Edmonds, unlike Lamb, has been a party to the conspiracy, if by that use of such an emotive term is meant public school, Oxbridge, Middlesex and England. The difference is that Edmonds has carried the colour and commonwealth of his colonialism with him. He is essentially an Edwardian figure constantly on a big game shoot. But, Edmonds does have a point, and it was brought home to me quite forcibly in Trinidad during the Fourth Test in 1986 when my taxi-driver gave me a lecture about 'whiteism' in cricket: 'First, you wouldn't give us Test status. Then you make us have a white captain. Then, when we're given equal status you still insist on whites being in our side, and finally, when we produce the best side in the world you want to change the laws about fast bowling.' He was only reiterating what that great Marxist, historian, playwright and cricket-nut, C. L. R. James, had been saying for most of his life. James was one of life's originals, who lived out his final days in Brixton. He died in 1989, but I suspect his work and thinking on cricket will outlive most of the journeyman hacks and television commentators that comprise cricket correspondents in one form or other.

Recently I have also worn a television, as well as a publishing, hat. Cricket has, according to the TCCB, been undersold as a sporting event on television. In cash terms that is so, but in terms of a public service the BBC's commitment has been exemplary. Last year's Ashes series was over after the Fourth Test yet the BBC continued to cover the two dead Tests. I wouldn't have bothered. They carried no interest to the public at large. At best they were worth a highlights package in the evening. Now Sky Television has already muscled in on cricket and I imagine that the BBC will look to Sky as a new partner in the 1990s. If Lord's is to retain its advantage in the new era of television, it needs, I think, to originate its own television signal. For, moan as we do sometimes about selectors, selection and South Africa, the thinking at Lord's has always been ahead of its counterparts – football and rugby.

I guess my feelings about Lord's are at best ambivalent. I love the cricket. At least, I love the Test matches. I'm not overly fussed about cold-hearted Middlesex and believe their future commercial success lies in seeking new accommodation. But that's an aside. I'm addicted to Test match cricket. Nothing has pleased me more these past six summers than seeing David Gower hit an exquisite square cut for four. His play has had a timeless quality about it. He was beaten up badly by the press in 1989 and let down dreadfully by the mob, but he's a survivor. We'll not see his like again. Youngsters with his talent will play golf. And then there was Ian Botham, the lionheart. His presence went beyond cricket. When he walked down the short flight of stairs to that white gate on to Lord's the crowd stopped. Time stopped. There was expectation, excitement and fear all around. It was like being at a Bruce Springsteen concert. Botham was electric. He has had a small self-destruct button but he's survived his mauling at the hands of the media – all lesser human beings – better than George Best, his soccer equivalent of the late 1960s. To me, Botham was Roy of the Rovers. And nowhere more than at Lord's.

Patrick Eagar is the doyen of cricket photographers and hates changing medium and working with words. Nevertheless, he was brave enough to do so and write about the particular problems and pleasures of being a Lord's lensman.

A Lens Too Small

PATRICK EAGAR

As an amateur photographer on the tightest of schoolboy budgets, the one thing I had never owned was a telephoto lens. I wanted to photograph cricket, and I had even experimented (with some success) in taking photographs through my father's binoculars; but the action was so far away, and my camera lens too small. The little white dots on my early cricket photographs were a source of constant frustration to me.

Then one day in 1963 – it was 24 June, a Monday – having somehow acquired enough money, I bought my first long lens. I was up at Cambridge and, taking the day off lectures, I caught the train to London. My first visit was to a Bond Street camera shop where I bought a modestly priced but reasonably powerful 400 mm lens. Then directly to Lord's, clutching my neatly wrapped purchase along with a camera that could be fitted to it. I settled down in the lower tier of the Warner Stand before play started. This, as it turned out, was just as well since five West Indian wickets fell for 15 runs in 6 overs.

The MCC signs posted round the ground were all too clear. 'No photography allowed,' they said, in that slightly imposing Lord's sort of way. You really were not meant to take photographs in those days because a Fleet Street agency called Sport & General used to do a deal with the MCC every year. They paid a sum and in return used to get exclusive access to all the matches at Lord's. And it was just that – exclusive; no one else got a look-in. The only way you could get a

187

camera into Lord's in those days was, as I had discovered, wrapped in sections in a Bond Street carrier bag.

Five wickets in 6 overs, the last – Charlie Griffith – bowled by Hampshire's Derek Shackleton who was playing in his first Test for years. Hampshire was and is very much my team, so it was all a bit much. Plenty of action and I had not even looked at my lens. Perhaps I could just get it out and use it as a sort of telescope, not really take any photographs, just look through it. They could not stop me doing that, could they? I really wanted to know what the magnifying effect of my new lens would be. Eventually I did get the lens out and, undetected, I did take some photographs, including the moment when Colin Cowdrey's arm was broken. However, they are misfiled somewhere and I have not seen them for years.

Most of my subsequent visits to Lord's have had the blessing of the authorities. In 1972 they opened the gates to bona fide professional photographers for the first time, and I have been back on a regular basis ever since. You can tell which photographs were taken in those early days. In the backgrounds there are no advertisements round the ground, the spectators are sprawled all over the grass, and there aren't as many photographers as you see today.

Some of the photographers in those days still used the long tom cameras designed and built in the 1920s and 1930s. These were ideally suited to cricket photography using good-quality aerial reconnaissance lenses. The best of them were salvaged from German cameras acquired after the First World War. The quality of the results, especially in good conditions, was, and still is, astounding. However, the cameras did suffer from two major disadvantages which hastened their eventual removal from the professional scene. First, once you had taken a photograph, it would be another twenty seconds or more (depending on the skill and dexterity of the photographer in reloading with a fresh plate) before you could take another. The second disadvantage was the sheer size and enormous weight of the things.

For this last reason I remember it was always a mistake to arrive at a match at the same time as Dennis Oulds from Central Press who was the last person to use one regularly at Lord's. If you had helped him up the three or four storeys of the Lord's Pavilion once you never forgot the experience. At the time there was a rule in force that photographers had to work from a different part of the ground on each day of a Test match. Poor Dennis would be hounded by various over-zealous officials who tried to ensure that he obeyed the rules and moved his overweight monster around the ground. This was clearly neither fair nor practical and in the end I think a truce was called. Once Dennis's lens was installed in the Pavilion he was allowed to leave it there. Eventually, just before his retirement, his employers bought him something more modern and manageable and the problem was resolved for ever.

My most ambitious project at Lord's was the attempt to photograph all the English and Australian cricketers who were present at the Lord's Centenary Test match in 1980. Over 240 had been invited to London for this match and I had hoped it would be possible to photograph them all in one group.

Many factors conspired against this. Some of the Australians developed an ailment more usually found in India and such places (though I do remember the Pakistani team were once reported to have had problems following an outing to a fish and chip shop in Grimsby). This 'bug' eliminated such names as Lindwall, Fingleton and Harvey.

Sir Donald Bradman had not come over for the celebrations; and in spite of as much lobbying as I could undertake, a fair number of English players failed to turn up in time for the photograph on the Friday morning. One English fast bowler even watched the whole performance from the BBC commentary box. Thanks to the imaginative and skilled organizational assistance of Col. Stephenson, then Assistant Secretary, we had marked out the exact area required at the Nursery End following a practice at the same spot a few weeks beforehand. The cameras were in place by 8.30 a.m. and it was a question of watching the London rain clouds roll up. As the gloom increased Jim Fairbrother, the groundsman, ordered his staff to move the covers on to the wicket, which somewhat spoiled the background to the photograph; but it did enable one more (future) Test cricketer to be included in the photograph – Norman Cowans, who was at the time on the Lord's groundstaff.

My anxiety was that there would not be enough light to take the photograph on the large-scale 5 × 4 in camera needed for a high-quality result. Should we cancel? There was little chance of reassembling the group, so we decided to carry on unless it poured.

The rain held off. Col. Stephenson put everyone in exactly the right places and there was time for me to take just six exposures. I had under-estimated the problems involved in getting 164 men to stare into the camera simultaneously. They were far too interested in chatting away to each other. Only the first two photographs were acceptable; the remainder began to look more and more like a successful cocktail party, with fewer and fewer faces pointing in my direction.

Yet the effort was worth it. More players would have been even better – Sir Donald Bradman would have been a bonus. However, I am still happy that the night before I persuaded Bill Bowes to come along; that Richie Benaud could take time from the BBC television schedules; that Andrew Sandham, wielding a white stick, and the almost immo-bile Percy Fender could cross the ground and sit for me. It was an hist-oric moment.

Amit Roy, *a senior feature writer on the staff of the* Sunday Times *in London, offers an Indian view of Imperial Lord's.*

Indian Summer

AMIT ROY

India unexpectedly won the Prudential World Cup on 25 June 1983 by beating West Indies in the final at Lord's. In a low-scoring match, the Indians, put in to bat by Clive Lloyd, the West Indian captain, managed only 183. However, the West Indies, who had started the match as easy favourites, were themselves bundled out for 140, giving India victory by 43 runs.

These, briefly, constitute what might be called the facts of the case; but they provide no understanding of why, for India at least, the win marked an historic occasion at Lord's. The firecrackers which exploded throughout India that evening were unsurprising expressions of joy. But even by the standards of sub-continental rhetoric, the response of Indian commentators to what was frankly a fluke victory seemed a trifle exaggerated. Some called it Indian cricket's finest hour; others insisted it was Indian sport's finest hour. One group even described it as the country's greatest day since independence from Britain at the 'stroke of midnight hour' on 14 August 1947.

I was working at the time for the *Daily Mail* in London, and had gone to Poland to cover a visit by Pope John Paul II to his native country. I was also stringing for an English-language daily in Calcutta called the *Amrita Bazar Patrika*. When India, against all odds, entered the final, I left the Pope in Cracow and caught the first available flight to London – and Lord's. Gossip had it that press tickets were so scarce that even the Nawab of Pataudi had been refused one (this turned out to be untrue for I later saw the former Indian captain in the press box). I managed to get one, thanks to the intervention of a friend, Tony Fleming, who at that time managed the MCC indoor cricket school at Lord's. When I arrived at the ground I was perturbed to be told that 'Amit Roy has already signed in'. I discovered an enterprising Indian journalist had obtained another ticket in my name. The culprit smiled broadly, not in the least embarrassed. The Indian crowds were mostly outside the ground, looking sad and waiting in vain for tickets. These were sold out months previously when few had thought India would figure in the final. Even Kapil Dev, the Indian captain, later admitted, 'A lot of people rang me from Bombay and said, "We are flying in to support you." But I had to tell them I couldn't get them in.'

Filled with 25,000 spectators, Lord's looked lovely on a perfect summer's day. India's start, though, was disastrous. Sunil Gavaskar went for only 2. The most productive over for India came when Krishnamachari Srikkanth hooked Andy Roberts, the West Indian fast bowler, for 4, and followed it with a pull for 6 and a straight-driven boundary. Srikkanth was out for a modest 38, but this turned out to be the highest individual tally in the match. By lunch, India were 100 for 4.

In contrast to the meagre Indian presence, West Indian spectators had arrived in impressive numbers, prepared for a day's serious drinking and confident of winning the World Cup. When Indian wickets started tumbling, the West Indians in the crowd applauded every run. They wanted their side to win, of course, but they also desired a decent contest to extend drinking time.

I made copious notes but should confess at this point that my match report never made it to my Indian paper. There had been a monsoon downpour in Calcutta and the streets outside the ancient *Amrita Bazar Patrika* building had, as usual, flooded, which disrupted the telex lines. Despite valiant attempts by the telex operators at Lord's, they just could not get my copy through – which was just as well.

This is because immediately after India were bowled out for 183, I sat down and hammered out an early report predicting a West Indian victory. It began: 'There was a purple flag in the crowd. It said, "West Indies cricket champions". And so indeed it proved to be.' Just as I handed this to the telex operator, Vivian Richards, who was taking the Indian bowling apart, was caught by Kapil Dev off Madan Lal for 33. In retrospect, Kapil identified this as the turning point of the match. I missed the catch but saw Kapil disappear into an Indian crowd on the boundary. A Pakistani reporter, Khalid Hassan, who used to be press secretary to Zulfikar Ali Bhutto, the former Pakistani Prime Minister, rolled his eyes – a sub-continental signal meaning strange things might now happen. I roughed out a possible new start to my story. This was: 'After early shocks, the West Indies coasted to a comfortable win. . . .'

Desmond Haynes went for 13; Larry Gomes for 5; Lloyd was caught by Kapil off Roger Binny's bowling for 8. I typed another start: 'West Indies snatched victory from the jaws of defeat. . . .' India, I told myself, would somehow blow it in the end, and wrote an angry introduction: 'India snatched defeat from the jaws of victory. . . .' As more wickets fell – Faoud Bacchus for 8, Jeffrey Dujon for 25, and Malcolm Marshall for 18 – I hesitated to adopt the line which seemed increasingly likely.

But at 7.28 p.m. (this was 2 minutes to the magical midnight hour in India, given the 4½ hour time difference), with the shadows lengthening across the ground and exultant Indians gathering in front of the Pavilion, an over-emotional reporter could give expression to the sentiments that had been forming in his subconscious: 'Incredibly, unbelievably, India are the new world champions.' The next morning the *Amrita Bazar Patrika* published an agency report of the match because my copy suffered the indignity of being sent by post. The paper was misguided and indulgent enough to publish it several days later.

In the dressing room, Kapil held court. 'Back home,' he ventured, 'they must be going crazy.' It was a little crazy in the dressing room as well, with normal conversation submerged by the sound of exploding champagne corks. Mohinder Amarnath, named man of the match after scoring 26 and taking 3 wickets, was sure that in India his father, Lala Amarnath, the former Indian Test cricketer, had followed every word of live radio commentary (in common with hundreds of millions of Indians). 'He must be very proud,' said Amarnath. The very happy Indian High Commissioner, Sayeed Mohammad, told the large gathering of Indian dignitaries packed into the dressing room, 'This is bound to affect the prestige of India in every way.'

For many Indians in Britain, the World Cup victory touched deep nationalistic roots. Outside Lord's, two Sikh youths honked their car horn as they passed a young English woman on the pavement. 'We are the world champions,' they shouted. 'We've won the World Cup.' She looked puzzled, shrugged her shoulders and walked on. But an elderly English couple in a passing car obviously understood for they nodded and smiled.

At a diplomatic dinner party shortly afterwards, a BBC man commented, 'It must be lovely for you Indians to listen to the sound of English cricket writers eating their own words.' It was true that the English cricket writers, normally the fairest and most knowledgeable of sports journalists, had not qualified their predictions for the final. In *The Times*, for example, John Woodcock said on the morning of the big match, 'No one in his right mind will confidently expect them [India] to win.' His report was titled: 'No place in the sun for the princely, underdog willow-wallahs of India'. Peter Smith, my former colleague at the *Daily Mail*, wrote, 'I can't see anything stopping Lloyd getting his hands on the trophy again.' Only *The Guardian*'s Frank Keating had a premonition: 'Indian legend on the cards.' To be fair, *The Times* later made amends with a report headlined: 'The bewitching hour when an Indian legend was born'. Woodcock rose to the occasion and said that India had not only won the World Cup but had 'captured the hearts of the cricket world as well. What happened will become a cricket legend.'

To cricket-lovers in India, Lord's evokes images which are all the more powerful because anecdotes about the hallowed turf, which most of them will never see, grow in the telling. As a little boy, for example, I was brought up in India in a small Bihar town called Patna. I had a friend, who had an elder brother, who had a friend, whose cousin had visited Lord's where he had seen Vijay Manjrekar, a stylish Indian batsman, execute a late cut. My friend gave us a demonstration of the shot being played at Lord's. Us yokels gaped open-mouthed. Lord's was that kind of place. Two days after the Indian victory, I bought my two-year-old son, Rajah, his first cricket bat. Today, when visitors from India come to London, they often make a point of going to Lord's or even just driving past it. It's a sort of pilgrimage.

And now a trio of Thespians. I see Rix, Pinter and Fry as my fast-bowling attack, though as cricketers that is not what they are. Stephen Fry, reassuringly fogeyish in many ways yet still one of the newish wave of 'alternative' comedians, writes: 'My cricketing career is about as distinguished as Andrew Lloyd Webber's trousers, I'm afraid. It has been one of prep school scorer; played for House Under 16s XI at school (once); then taught for a year at a prep school, specializing in creative umpiring and teaching boys the difference between a half-volley and a yorker. Since then, village cricket (occasionally) and ad hoc teams. Highest score, 18; most wickets in a match, 2. Feeble, isn't it; but, by Christ, I love the game and that's what counts.'

What more can one say?

The Great Lie

STEPHEN FRY

Lord's! The very word is an anagram of 'sordl'. The Headquarters of cricket. The acre or so of green velvet nestling in the warm folds of St Johnners Wood. The acre (itself an anagram of 'hectare') that is girlfriend, mistress, mother, casual boyfriend, sergeant major, nursemaid, father-confessor and one-night stand all rolled into one. All rolled into one by the heavy roller of memory, on the square of reminiscence; that square that slopes slightly at one end, assisting the deviating swing of recall that causes the ball of thought to cut away from the norm of reality and catch the outside edge of fantasy that is snapped up by the cupped hands of fate.

Lawks! 'Each article should be crisp and to the point, elegant without being too elegiac, and firmly rooted in first-hand personal experience.' There's a thing. I fear that in my opening paragraph I may just have been guilty of overstepping the mark. In these austere times the purple Cardus gets shown the yellow card. Time to crispen up. My first-hand experience of Lord's began as second-hand experience when, an engaging youngster with important new strains of impetigo and hair that could oil a Harrow-sized Stuart Surridge Special, I picked up *Psmith In The City* by P. G. Wodehouse. This masterly work, after *Ulysses* and the invention of the electric under-duvet quite possibly the most important achievement of the twentieth century, contains a scene in which Mike Jackson, last and greatest of the cricketing Jacksons, is called upon to make up the numbers at a Lord's cricket match. Keats had a dash at explaining what he felt like when first peeping into Chapman's *Homer* – he said that he felt like some watcher of the skies who sees a new planet swimming into his ken: the experience, he went on to relate, wasn't so very unlike that of fat Cortez standing to the west of the Darien Gap and looking at the Pacific for the first time. I've not read Chapman's *Homer*. Don't ask me why: pressure of time; always been meaning to; never quite got round to it; promise it's first on the list for my next holiday, etc., etc.; but I can assure you that *Psmith In The City* caused feelings in me by no means dissimilar to those which animated the bosom of John Keats.

'Lor!' I said to myself. From that day to this Lord's cricket has exerted the most powerful influence over my being. But there's many a slip 'twixt wicket-keeper and gully. The influence has been, let us be quite clear about this, an entirely fantastic one. Let me attempt, in my fumbling way, to explain. Imagination, Iris Murdoch once remarked, in that way she has, is a creative force that comes from the individual soul: fantasy, she went sternly on to asseverate, is a non-creative force; it comes from the imagination of others. My fascination with Lord's is a result entirely of the fascination of others. There is a literature, a lore and a pre-selected attitude to Lord's already in place. That is what I have been seduced by.

Lore! That is what has done it. Let's be honest. It's a cricket ground less beautiful than many – Worcester and Adelaide spring to mind as more charming venues – whose place as an English cultural icon owes much to the eccentricity and absurdity of its foundation, the weirdness of the cricketing Lords who determine the laws and direction of cricket from its Long Rooms and Galleries, and the heraldic peculiarities that surround the institution – Old Father Time, the irrelevant 'Marylebone' appellation of the society that uses the ground as its clubroom, the grotesque flame-like colourings of that club, the preposterous jacket and tie rules, the necessary spectre of spotted dick and starched nannies that is raised by the ground's 'Nursery', and, oh, a hundred other wild and wonderful details that serve to create a flavouring and an atmosphere that is consonant with our law courts, our constitution,

our royalty, our great universities, public schools, gentlemen's clubs and other dotty splendours. 'What is your idea of heaven?' 'The Saturday afternoon of an Ashes match at Lord's.' 'What is your idea of hell?' 'The M25 on a Tuesday in February.' Lord's proffers an attainable paradise whose joy is entirely tribal. We are *told* that Lord's is heaven, it's our heaven, a British heaven. If you can't accommodate this view of the place then you are seven kinds of stinker. Those are the laws.

Laws! Cricket has laws, not rules, and I'm prepared to obey them all. I'll be subversive, imaginative and independent three hundred and sixty days of the year, creating my paradise and my own sodalities; but when it comes to cricket I join in the common fantasy. I sit watching the white Druids waving their juju sticks and I worship at the common shrine. For five days I *belong* to this silly country with its silly vanities, injustices, bigotries and cruelties. The whole crowd of spectators are my friends and we share a common secret, a common advantage over everyone else on the globe. I say to myself, 'I'm *here!* To my left there's the famous clock, to my right the famous scoreboard, on the famous field are the famous players and I am part of the famous crowd on this famous first day of what will be this famous match.' I'm playing the game and I like it. Like Mike Jackson I'm playing at Lord's. I'm playing at being English. It's ludicrous, but then that's what ludicrous means: playing the game. I once sat next to Mick Jagger watching David Gower make a hundred against Australia. Can't get no greater satisfaction than that, now can you?

Lord's! It isn't in London, it's in the mind, the collective unconscious of the British, like the Old Course at St Andrews and the village fête. Lord's isn't cricket; it has little to do with the multiplicity of physical talents and tactical thinking that make up the game, a game better expressed on a beach in Barbados or coconut matting in Colombo. Lord's is an opportunity for a certain kind of Englishman to leave the world of edge-of-town shopping and Trust House Forté conference suites and dive headfirst into a beautiful, shameless, disgraceful, delightful and ludicrous lie.

The following piece is essentially an anecdote from Sir Brian Rix's autobiography. Rix is famous for his Whitehall farces and for his indefatigable work for the charity Mencap. He was president of the Lord's Taverners in 1970.

Hall of Fame

BRIAN RIX

In the second part of my autobiography, *Farce About Face* (published in 1989 by Hodder & Stoughton), I told the tale of the second time I was caught as the subject of 'This Is Your Life'. It was at Her Majesty's Theatre in the Haymarket on 22 March 1977. I should explain that I once played cricket for Hull in the Yorkshire League, for the MCC, the Stage and the Lord's Taverners. Because of this, the final guest to be whisked on was that magnificent West Indian fast bowler, Wes Hall. Or, to give him his present full title, Senator Wesley Hall, Minister for Tourism and Sport in Barbados. How did he come to grace the programme? Well, I first met him way back in 1963 when he and Charlie Griffith were striking terror into the hearts of England's cricketers. Our paths had crossed on a number of occasions since then, particularly in a match at Lord's in June 1973, when Wes and I joined Elton John, David Frost, Gerald Harper, Michael Parkinson, Peter Cook, Ed Stewart and Ray Barratt in a team organized by Vic Lewis to do battle with Middlesex in aid of Fred Titmus's benefit. I must report that in my fortieth year, I took 2 for 30, made 23 not out, and held a blinding catch at backward point, which brought the crowd to its feet and me a bruised hand which had to be seen to be believed. For weeks I bored everyone with the story, which became more and more exaggerated as time wore on. In the end, Wes Hall had delivered the ball at about 90 m.p.h. to Mike Brearley, who thumped it at about 140 m.p.h. to my right, whence I dived and came up clutching the ball, which miraculously had stuck to my hand. In fact, I think the batsman was Norman Featherstone and the bowler Ed Stewart, but it makes a better story my way. And it *was* travelling at 140 m.p.h., in either version – and I *did* catch it with one hand. So there!

When that particular match was over, I was invited into that holy of holies at Lord's – the Committee Room. I explained that my daughter, Louisa, was with me, but they decided to bend the rules and allow her to accompany me. One of the old boys came up to her, as she sipped her sherry, and guffawed: 'You know, my dear, it's a great privilege for you to be here. Normally the only women allowed in are the Queen and the cleaners.' One of the great bastions of chauvinism is Lord's. No wonder Her Majesty only goes once a year.

And what about His Honour, Wesley Hall? Well, some three years earlier, Elspet and I were winging our way to the Coral Reef Hotel in Barbados in the company of Leslie and Jean Crowther. 'Lucky devils' you may think, but we were going out with a solemn duty in mind: to support our ailing Test team in the Third Test at Bridgetown. Every day during the five days of the Test, small groups of enthusiasts, the four of us amongst them, left our hotels and proceeded by bumpy bus to the ground, there to cheer on the English team. We had a job on the Saturday: with 20,000 people crammed into a ground holding 14,000, a handful of English – even with loud voices like Leslie's and mine – found it difficult to be heard above the din.

We had another noisy reception of a more pleasant kind when Leslie and I did a cabaret at our hotel for the team and their supporters. Several hundred squeezed into a space normally holding less than one hundred, but they were a marvellous audience and we both found difficulty coming off that cramped cabaret floor! Next day we marched up and down the beach proudly receiving plaudits from all and sundry, and as our team went on to achieve a noble draw we felt we must have raised morale somehow. Our morale was considerably lifted, too, for our guide and mentor in Barbados was the very same Wes Hall, and going round the island with him was royal progress, indeed. Thus, three years later, thanks to 'This Is Your Life', we had a chance to repay his hospitality. We took it with both hands. Wes came to stay with us for the rest of his time in London, and we had a marvellous party. It lasted for four days!

Harold Pinter's contribution first appeared in 1969 but seemed to me worth a revival. I like the idea of our greatest living playwright playing hooky from drama school for a Lord's Test. Proper sense of priority. He told me the story himself, complete with actions, in a hotel room in Toronto while I was preparing this book, and I couldn't resist it. He plays for a famous team, the Gaieties, and has written a compelling monograph about his most illustrious team-mate, the late Arthur Wellard, the Somerset bowler and six-hitter.

Hutton and the Past

HAROLD PINTER

Hardstaff and Simpson at Lord's. Notts versus Middlesex. 1946 or 1947. After lunch, Keeton and Harris had opened for Notts. Keeton swift, exact, interested; Harris Harris. Harris stonewalled five balls in the over for no particular reason and hit the sixth for six, for no particular reason. Keeton and Harris gave Notts a fair start. Stott, at number three, smacked the ball hard, was out in the early afternoon. Simpson joined Hardstaff. Both very upright in their stance. They surveyed the field, surveyed themselves, began to bat.

The sun was strong, but calm. They settled into the afternoon, no hurry, all in order. Hardstaff clipped to mid-wicket. They crossed. Simpson guided the ball between mid-off and the bowler. They crossed. Their cross was a trot, sometimes a walk, they didn't need to run. They placed their shots with precision, they knew where they were going. Bareheaded. Hardstaff golden. Simpson dark. Hardstaff off-drove, silently, Simpson to deep square leg. Simpson cut. Hardstaff cut, finer. Simpson finer. The slips, Robertson, Bennett, attentive. Hardstaff hooked, immaculate, no sound. They crossed, and back. Deep square leg in the heat after it. Jim Sims on at the Pavilion End with leg-breaks. Hardstaff wristed him into the covers. Simpson to fine leg.

Two. Sims twisting. Hardstaff wristed him into the covers, through the covers, fielder wheeling, for four. Quite unhurried. Seventy in 90 minutes. No explosions. Batsmanship. Hardstaff caught at slip, off Sims.

Worrell and Weekes at Kingston upon Thames. 1950. The Festival. Headley had flicked, showed what had been and what remained of himself, from the 1930s. Worrell joined Weekes with an hour to play. Gladwin and Jackson bowling. Very tight, very crisp, just short of a length, jolting, difficult. Worrell and Weekes scored 90 before close of play. No sixes, nothing off the ground. Weekes smashed, red-eyed, past cover, smashed to long leg, at war, met Gladwin head-on, split mid-wicket in two, steel. Worrell wanted to straight-drive to reach his 50. Four men at the sight-screen to stop him. He straight-drove, pierced them, reached his 50. Gladwin bowled a stinging ball, only just short, on middle and leg. Only sensible course was to stop it. Worrell jumped up, both feet off, slashed it from his stomach, square-cut for four, boundary first bounce.

MCC versus Australians. Lord's, 1948. Monday. On the Saturday the Australians had plastered the MCC bowling, Barnes 100, Bradman just short. On Monday morning Miller hit Laker for five sixes into the Tavern. The Australians passed 500 and declared. The weather darkened. MCC 30 minutes' batting before lunch. The Australians came into the field chucking the ball hard at each other, broad, tall, sure. Hutton and Robertson took guard against Lindwall and Miller. Robertson caught Tallon off Miller. Lindwall and Miller very fast. The sky black. Edrich caught Tallon off Miller. Last ball before lunch. MCC 20 for 2.

After lunch the Australians, arrogant, jocular, muscular, larking down the Pavilion steps. They waited, hurling the ball about, eight feet tall. Two shapes behind the Pavilion glass. Frozen, before emerging, a split second. Hutton and Compton. We knew them to be the two greatest English batsmen. Down the steps together, out to the middle. They played. The Australians quieter, wary, tight. Bradman studied them. They stayed together for an hour before Compton was out, and M. P. Donnelly, and Hutton, and the Australians walked home.

First Test at Trent Bridge. The first seven in the English batting order: Hutton, Washbrook, Edrich, Compton, Hardstaff, Barnett,

Yardley. They'll never get them out, I said. At lunch on the first day, England 78 for 8.

Hutton.

England versus New Zealand, 1949. Hutton opened quietly, within himself, setting his day in order. At the first hour England 40 for none. Hutton looking set for a score. Burtt, slow left hand, took the ball at the Nursery End, tossed it up. To his first ball Hutton played a superb square drive to Wallace at deep point. Wallace stopped it. The crowd leaned in. Burtt again. Hutton flowed into another superb square drive to Wallace's right hand. Wallace stopped it. Back to the bowler. Burtt again, up. Hutton, very hard a most brilliant square drive to Wallace's left hand. Wallace stopped it. Back to the bowler. The crowd. Burtt in, bowled. Hutton halfway up the pitch immediately, driving straight. Missed it. Clean bowled. On his heel back to the Pavilion.

Hutton was never dull. His bat was part of his nervous system. His play was sculptured. His forward defensive stroke was a complete statement. The handle of his bat seemed electric. Always, for me, a sense of his vulnerability, of a very uncommon sensibility. He never just went through the motions, nothing was glibly arrived at. He was never, for me, as some have defined him, simply a 'master technician'. He attended to the particular but rarely lost sight of the context in which it took place. But one day in Sydney he hit 37 in 24 minutes and was out last ball before lunch when his bat slipped in hitting a further four, when England had nothing to play for but a hopeless draw, and he's never explained why he did *that*. I wasn't there to see it and probably regret that as much as anything. But I wasn't surprised to hear about it, because every stroke he made surprised me.

I heard about Hutton's 37 on the radio. 7 a.m. Listened to every morning of the 1946–7 series. Alan McGilvray talking. Always England six wickets down and Yardley 35 not out. But it was in an Irish kitchen in County Galway that, alone, I heard Edrich and Compton in 1953 clinch the Ashes for England.

Those were the days of Bedser and Wright, Evans, Washbrook and Gimblett, M. P. Donnelly, Smailes and Bowes, A. B. Sellers, Voce and Charley Barnett, A. W. Wellard, S. M. Brown and Jim Sims, Mankad, Mustaq Ali, Athol Rowan, even H. T. Bartlett, even Hammond and certainly Bradman.

One morning at drama school I pretended illness and, pale and shaky, walked into Gower Street. Once round the corner I jumped on a bus and ran into Lord's at the Nursery End to see through the terraces Washbrook late cutting for four, the ball skidding towards me. That beautiful evening Compton made 70.

But it was 1950 when G. H. G. Doggart missed Walcott at slip off Edrich, and Walcott went on to score 165, Gomez with him. Christiani was a very good fielder. Ramadhin and Valentine had a good season. Hutton scored 202 not out against them and against Goddard bowling breakbacks on a bad wicket at The Oval.

It was 1949 when Bailey caught Wallace blindingly at silly mid-on. And when was it I watched Donnelly score 180 for the Gents versus Players? He went down the afternoon with his lightning pulls.

Constantine hitting a six over fine leg into the Pavilion. Talk of a schoolboy called May.

And finally, for symmetry and because J. L. Carr is surely right about verse (along with cricket) being England's true glory, another poem. Brand-new this time. Gavin Ewart, who wrote it, once took wickets bowling underarm at Wellesley House, Broadstairs, Kent, a famous cricketing prep school which produced father and son, Frank and George Mann, both England captains, as well as all the Cowdreys. Ewart says, 'I prefer Lord's to The Oval, and most of my adult cricket-watching has been done there.' Which seems a good note on which to end. . . .

'Lord's in the Fifties'

GAVIN EWART

Sitting on the Mound Stand
   behind the bowler's arm,
I saw most of summer,
   and summer has its charm –
like criss-crossing couples
   in a dance the batsmen run,
it was furious but fun
under the summer sun.

It was May and Cowdrey,
   Griffith, Hall and Close,
Edrich and Compton –
   sweet as Athole brose!*
Truman scaring Indians,
   it was Statham kept the boat
very steadily afloat –
and Laker, wily stoat!

* Athole brose is whisky mixed with honey and oatmeal

It was Lord's, the fifties,
    ice-cream cones for tea –
a lunchtime pint of Guinness
    and sandwiches for me!
Binoculars and scorecards
    and batsmen at the crease,
    a Saturday release,
    a rustic kind of peace!

Not a part of London –
    but like a village green
(though somehow more important)
    transported to the scene
from days when earls and yeomen
    used bats that looked like clubs,
    a land with inns (not pubs)
    where foxes kept their cubs!

A bow tie, orange/yellow,
    elegant and grand –
strolling in the garden,
    lordly in the stand –
marks dandies in the Long Room;
    and the reminiscent bar
    brings the ghosts from far –
    but shining like a star!

Biting through a sandwich,
    I didn't want to be
part of that part-sad élite;
    but, happy to be me,
I could enter that existence
    where no offices exist –
    just the ball, the jerk and twist
    of the spinner's wrist!

Where the batsmen pick the wrong 'un,
    the Bosie – or the mock
is put on them by experts
    such as Tony Lock.
My Shangri-la, you'd call it,
    a lifeline from a life
    where strain and strife
    cut like a knife!